PAIN-FREE

EASY STEPS TO A HAPPIER, HEALTHIER

YOU

SOPHIA KUPSE

For more information please visit: **www.themusclewhisperer.co.uk**

Painless Publishing

ISBN-13:978-1537225005

DEDICATION

For all those who suffer with any form of Autism, Mental Health, Dementia & Alzheimer's. You battle every day through a confusing world, that seems to misunderstand your beautiful, talented gifts. You are ahead of us mere mortals. I have been blessed to work with you and am richer in my life for knowing you all.

CONTENTS

ACKNOWLEDGMENTS

DAVID CLARKE, ROCK PR – For always believing in me

MAX MORRIS, WWW.MILKBAR CREATIVE.COM – For having the patience to put book three together

MY FAMILY – For keeping your cool when I lost mine, you always inspire me

INTRODUCTION

In my first book **The Muscle Whisperer** – The keys to Unlocking Your Back Pain, I looked at how the physical body held onto emotional pain and I gave easy step-by-step solutions, through diet and movement, which could help resolve it. The book received great reviews and a huge positive response, so I decided to look further into how the mind creates physical pain using further research.

Book two, **Desperately Seeking A Pain-Free Self**, focused more on the connection of how the thoughts and inner conversations we have with ourselves, lead to chemical changes in the body, that eventually create physical pain.

I also looked at the relationship we have between the adult and inner child within ourselves, which connects in our conscious and unconscious mind. Again, this ultimately leads to our pain and I offer proven methods that help ease and resolve the discomfort.

In this - my new book **Pain-Free Easy Steps To a Happier Healthier You**, I look more deeply into how we learned this process of pain, from our birth to our latter years; how key challenges and events that are stored in our unconscious mind eventually release unexplained pain. Even though every chapter will relate to a specific decade or decades, the information in it can be applied to any point of your life right now, no matter what age you currently are.

This book will help you see pain from all your past years, as well as looking ahead to decades you have not yet reached, so you can stop the build-up of unnecessary pain. The saying goes: "Forearmed is forewarned". Pain can be controlled, reduced and even prevented, using easy, proven ways to restore your wellbeing in mind and body.

This book offers an answer to the never-ending question of why you suffer so much mental and physical pain. This is just one piece of the huge jigsaw puzzle on what causes pain, but it could be the missing piece that helps you understand it better and finally gives you natural pain relief that lasts. This could be the link that you have been looking for, that explains why you have your pain. This book will also question how responsible are you as an individual, in contributing to your pain, when no accident, trauma or injury is to blame, and when medics cannot offer you an answer, after numerous tests have shown negative results.

The Growing Need to Understanding Pain

In my quest to unravel how our emotions create our physical pain, it dawned on me that no matter how I explained the treatment I founded - LT Therapy, the technique that resets muscle memory in order to reduce pain and restore wellbeing in the mind and body, there are still people out there, (including my extremely logical-minded brother) who can understand the link, but cannot process beyond the concept.

In order to do that, you have to take responsibility and acknowledge that your daily thinking pattern contributes to how you feel. In other words, from the moment you wake up you are thinking; you can either choose happy thoughts, by looking forward to all the good stuff the day has to offer, or miserable thoughts. You know the type, about your 'going nowhere' job, the boring traffic, what you want to wear, but can't because your never-ending diet, the one you keep failing at, stops you getting into your favourite jeans, the pair you wore a decade ago and still hope to get into now.

Negative thinking like this, will most definitely set you up for a depressing day I guarantee you. When a person can no longer put up with their endless bouts of neck and shoulder pain or lower back pain, they finally allow themselves to invest in any treatment that brings them some kind of relief to ease their pain. But why do you wait till you are at the end of your tether to seek help?

The treatment I founded - LT Therapy - is a therapy in two parts, verbal memory release, as well as physical muscle memory release. The recipient has to engage on a journey of looking back into their own past, including their childhood, which for most of us is too painful a trip and one we prefer not to think about. However, when done in this way, the person allows themselves to talk about their trapped emotions. As I am neutral, I don't judge them for past decisions they made. I am their therapist. They trust and value my expertise, as I gently guide them through their dark tunnel and they come out safely at the other end. By linking what specific memories you are accessing from your conscious or unconscious mind, using my years of experience and intuition, LT Therapy finds the connection of that memory, held in the body and frees it.

Using its unique three-way system of Volcanic heat, ice marble and manipulation, it resets the muscle memory. Is this a proven pathway, you may ask. Yes, is my reply. But how, you question.

The Healing Value of 'Hot & Cold' Therapy

Here comes the history and science bit, but don't worry it's not too heavy. Hydrotherapy, formerly called hydropathy, is a part of medicine and alternative medicine, in particular of naturopathy, occupational therapy and physiotherapy, that involves the use of water for pain relief and treatment. The term encompasses a broad range of approaches and therapeutic methods that take advantage of the physical properties of water, such as temperature and pressure, for healing purposes, to stimulate blood circulation and treat the symptoms of certain diseases. Various therapies used in present-day hydrotherapy employ water jets, underwater massage and mineral baths (e.g. balneotherapy and thalassotherapy) and/or whirlpool baths, hot Roman baths, hot tubs, Jacuzzis, cold plunge and mineral baths. If you've experienced any of these, you will have felt the benefits. Hydrotherapy uses the application of hot and cold, using packs, hot air and steam baths, baths of hot water and cold, hot and cold bandages (or compresses).

Various forms of hydrotherapy have been recorded in ancient Egyptian, Persian, Greek and Roman civilisations. Egyptian royalty bathed with essential oils and flowers, while Romans had communal public baths for their citizens. Hypocrites prescribed bathing in spring water for sickness. Other cultures noted for a long history of hydrotherapy include China and Japan, the latter being centred primarily around Japanese hot springs. Many such histories predate the Roman thermae, their large imperial bath complexes, as one of the primary sources of hydrotherapy to treat medical conditions. Today's modern medicine successes, particularly with drug therapy, removed or replaced many water-related therapies from the mid-20th century.

While the physiological mechanisms were initially poorly understood, the therapeutic benefits have long been recognised, even if the reason for the therapeutic benefit was in dispute. For example, in November 1881, the British Medical Journal noted that hydropathy was a specific instance, or "particular case", of general principles of thermodynamics. That is, "the application of heat and cold in general", as it applies to physiology, mediated by hydropathy. In 1883, another writer stated "Not, be it observed, that hydropathy is a water treatment after all, but that water is the medium for the application of heat and cold to the body".

The "active agents in the treatment (are) heat and cold", of which water is little more than the vehicle, and not the only one".

The National Centre of Biotechnology Information published a study on 6th May 2014 by A. Mooventhan and L. Nivethitha on 'Scientific Evidence-based Effects of Hydrotherapy on Various Systems of the Body.' The study wanted to bring together medical evidence to show how hydrotherapy, the use of water with hot and cold temperatures, healed the mind and body. The study showed that it was the elements of hot and cold, in whatever format, that had improved a multitude of medical conditions, ranging from improving immunity, pain management, fibromyalgia, chronic obstructive pulmonary diseases (COPD), asthma, fatigue, anxiety, obesity, hypercholesterolemia, hyperthermia, labour, to name a few.

The Science Behind LT Therapy

LT Therapy uses these two mediums, hot and cold, to reset muscle memory in the physical body. The heat side is retained in volcanic basalt stones. This volcanic rock (or lava) that characteristically is dark in colour, contains 45% to 54% silica and is rich in iron and magnesium. I use this natural creation to shift negative blockages held in the muscles. These feel like deep-rooted knots to clients, and are a by-product of their negative thinking. This negative state of mind leads to an over-production of adrenaline and cortisol, which, unused, store as lactic acid, embedding itself in-between layers of muscle, usually in the biggest muscle groups of the human anatomy, mainly in the neck, shoulders, mid and lower back.

The healing properties of this stone can penetrate extreme areas of tightness very quickly with little discomfort to the recipient. It diffuses pain, which lays dormant under trapped nerves and inflammation, caused by your natural tendency to engage in daily negative chatter. The gentle heat transcends into the muscle layers, discharging tense rigid areas, allowing rapid movement to be restored in the muscle.

Ice marble is the cold ingredient used in this three-part therapy. The finest, smoothest medical grade Carrera marble is a natural component that is able to retain temperatures below zero degrees, which are necessary for resetting muscle memory. As the heat discharges toxic waste held in the muscles, cold marble reinstates the muscle back to its soft natural texture. Manipulation is applied, in between working the hot/cold stones, allowing oxygenated blood and nutrients to feed and free the muscle. It's like breathing life back into an area that barely had a pulse.

LT Therapy Mapping System

Through the knowledge of my experience and wisdom from my intuition, I observe and gently apply pressure to the client's muscles, explaining as I go along, what their back says about their past, what they are holding onto.

I am able to do this through the mapping system I developed, a part of LT Therapy. As I move from muscle to muscle, the client confirms each area I cover matches their history.

To make it easier for you to grasp, let's compare it to another well-known and loved treatment. In reflexology, there is a mapping route on the feet that corresponds to the physical body. In LT Therapy, the neck, shoulders and back are the mapping system of the mind.

In order for muscle memory to operate, there are thousands of sensory nerves that lay under every muscle group of the body from head to toe. These sensory nerves communicate to a part of the brain called the cerebellum. Through procedural memory of the conscious mind, you learn everything, how to walk, talk, balance, ride a bike, sing, dance etc. Once you have learnt each new task, it drops into your unconscious mind, to run the job automatically. This is where muscle memory becomes the star of the show. The same sensory nerves that allow you to speak, balance and move are like a giant telephone exchange, enabling the physical body to move muscles automatically, whilst permitting your thoughts to be transmitted down the same sensory nerve pathway. So how you think suddenly become extremely important, as it begins to affect how you feel and, ultimately, your wellbeing.

In order to reset muscle memory, I focus on feeling for key areas that repeatedly become, for most people, the main offenders for pain. These are the shoulders, neck and lower back. When I press certain points in these muscles, they parallel how the conscious and unconscious mind converse. In other words, whenever you access your past or present memories relating to negative people or events in your life, you release adrenaline. If this remains unused, it converts to lactic acid which eventually gets stored in specific muscle groups corresponding to that person or thought. For instance, constant worry about your mother will tighten the muscle that sits below the neck and connects with the top of your shoulder on your right side. Apply pressure using your thumb and fingers in the corner of this shoulder and you will see how tight it can be.

Physical Pain Vs Emotions

Why does the same question continually get asked by people, when we already have the answer out there in science? How can our physical pain be created by our emotions?

The answer lies in muscle memory and how we view ourselves, but again and again, there are certain groups of people who find this concept difficult to accept, (as they find looking at themselves difficult), yet they believe there is definitely something in it. They choose instead, to always look for the physical reason why they are in pain, (remember no physical trauma or injury has happened, the pain just came on) as it's the easy option and the brain is set to default to this answer every time.

Why could they not grasp the basics of this simple model? Was it like the 'salts in the cupboard' analogy when you look in the cupboard and still can't see the salt, then someone comes along and hey presto! It was right in front of you all along, but you never saw it.

Maybe I am ahead of my time and in 20 years, western medicine will look back and agree with my approach to pain. I am not alone in this thinking. There are already others who believe the same. After all, it was years before the medical world accepted Alexander Fleming's discovery of penicillin and eventually he was given credit for his amazing discovery with a Nobel Prize!

As a child, I was always good at explaining things and I was a wonderful story-teller like my father. As I grew older, my love of fiction turned into a passion for factual information.

I am not here to preach or enforce my view. I simply want to offer another perspective at looking at pain. This is particularly aimed at those people who have ongoing pain, which medics cannot treat with a pill or diagnosis. It is not linked to a genetic illness or accident/physical trauma, but a physical pain that comes for no apparent reason. I have worked with such people for over 25 years and have seen amazing results with miraculous recoveries from all walks of life.

I have seen transformational results from people who were on long-term medication for pain relief that had ceased to work, forcing them to seek alternate solutions. Seeing so many people suffering on a daily basis (including my own family) with so much unnecessary pain, dependant on prescriptions that only partially eased it, was not good enough for me. I was determined to find a link to why in today's modern 21st century living, we were still struggling with this anomaly. In fact, our pain is growing at an alarming rate rather than decreasing.

Our Ongoing Battle With Pain

Pain can be your best friend or your worst enemy. It follows you throughout your life, whether you want it to or not. Pain that cannot be related to anything medical or physical is what I specialise in and why LT Therapy, the technique that resets muscle memory that I founded, has become a rapidly growing treatment experienced by hundreds of people worldwide.

It also helps people with a medical diagnosis ease their symptoms and dramatically reduce their pain. People need to know and understand why they feel such a variation in pain, so they can begin to heal. My treatment unlocks the door of their mind that stores the answer.

But why does this hidden pain affect people in so many different ways? Those who have very few health issues such as headaches, lower back pain, neck and shoulder pain and leg pain have introduced more balance in their life. They have worked out that when they feel less stressed, anxiety drops and they begin to enjoy the moment pain-free. They have learnt to work on themselves, to nurture and care for their total wellbeing – all of which starts in the mind.

When we control what we allow in our mind, our body responds well. When we become overwhelmed and time-poor, pain becomes the indicator to highlight that you need to make that change. It's telling you to slow down, take time off, use boundaries or you will suffer burnout or meltdown. Signs of this are sleep deprivation; addiction to processed foods, chocolate, alcohol, recreational or prescriptive drugs; poor motivation and referral pain in the body. These are all signs that you are burning the candle (that's yourself) at both ends. I've been there numerous times. When the body can't take it anymore, it will shut you down and you will have no control over that decision.

Your mind gives you numerous chances, opportunities to recognise the need for change, but you still ignore it. Minor changes lead to massive lifestyle benefits, but instead of listening to your mind, you decide to take the short cut, working to the edge and then boom! It blows your candle out with a complete shutdown. Then you panic and decide something is seriously wrong with you for your mind and body to suddenly stop working. Fearing it's something more serious, you run to the doctor for blood tests and scans. You need reassurance that it's not the big 'C' or early stages of heart disease or diabetes.

Instead results find nothing, possibly a deficiency in vitamin D or B. But you need something more tangible, some label to justify taking time out. It's easier to say it's ME (CFS) or fibromyalgia than to tell your friends that you did this to yourself.

These illnesses by the way are very real. I suffered from ME in my late twenties and successfully recovered, but the symptoms at the time were very real. Such illnesses are usually triggered by a build-up of stress or major event in your life, such as a divorce, bereavement or the birth of a baby.

By the time you are lying there in your bed, you've unconsciously given your body permission to release a tidal wave of pain in the form of lethargy, weakness, loss of appetite and physical aches. It's like unblocking the backlog of what you've been unknowingly racing towards, the dark side. This is the result of accumulated stress. When it is fully unleashed, it makes you feel painful and unattractive.

Instead of building a balanced life through mindfulness, meditation and gratitude, you went the opposite way. You became dependent on regular visits to the doctors to help you get out of the mess you got yourself in. You'll be offered antidepressants and painkillers - everything your body doesn't need. These will only suppress healing. It numbs the surface. That's why they don't work for many people. Your journey is to now focus on being the real and true you. It starts with you accepting and identifying that you are really okay. Your medical results prove it. You've only taken a wrong turn on the road of life. Now you can get back on track and make 'you' happen again.

Finding The Solution To Our Pain

Whilst researching this book, and understanding how stress and daily challenges can affect our pain, the two main factors that stood out in improving and reducing pain were physical movement and a healthy mind-set.

Based on hundreds of research papers, medical data and information from around the world, we know that the mind-body connection strongly exists. I discuss this in more detail in later chapters and specifically in chapter nine The Power of the Mind and Brain changes over the Decades.

We know that how we feel emotionally will 100% resonate in our physical body. When we feel happy, we feel good all over, thanks to those lovely, abundant, wholesome endorphins our body produces, which helps us heal.

When we feel negative, sad or stressed, our body releases chemicals such as adrenaline (the 'fight or flight' response system) which, when unused, leads to a build-up of lactic acid in the body and eventually pain.

With all this evidence proving that a healthy lifestyle - combing a balanced diet, daily exercise, positive thinking, meditation and holistic therapies - can we not take action to heal ourselves, rather than continuing to suffer?

Clearly, we don't love ourselves enough to maintain such a healthy programme on a daily basis. It is only when we are sick that we turn to these great healing tools, then we discard them after they have served their purpose.

Mind Body Pain

Pain not only affects the body, but also the mind. One of the leading reasons we suffer such pain is daily stress. Stress is needed to challenge our minds and stretch our development, but too much of it becomes negative and toxic, just like too much alcohol or a bad diet. Stress has been with us since time began. From the moment we are conceived we accepted it as part of our growth.

Chapter one covers this hypothesis in more detail. Based on the beliefs instilled in us by our parents from childhood, we rarely make the connection that our pain originates from then and even earlier. Not allowing ourselves to heal is all down to the relationship we have with ourselves; how we value and respect who we are and ultimately, how much we love and care for ourselves. These are critical in influencing our happiness.

When we suffer with back pain, for instance, our mobility is compromised, we feel down, moody and upset, and we can't enjoy the fruits of our labour, the joy that each day brings. Gripped in a world of pain, we buy into medication for short-term relief.

Western medication only buys our body temporary time to mask the pain. It suppresses our natural ability to heal and does not get to the root of the problem. To get to the root of each physical pain, we need to exam the original cause and this can go as far back as childhood and birth. For most of us, this is a journey too painful to do on our own, so we need the guidance of experts such as psychologists, holistic therapists, acupuncturists, hypnotherapists and healers. By giving yourself permission to break down the negative barriers that overpower the real you, you begin your journey of self-healing.

In the UK, we struggle to follow this route for fear of looking weak and being labelled weird. In the USA and Europe, they embrace talking therapies as they understand that living in today's world is extremely stressful and in order to counteract stress, we need to take care of the mind as well as the body.

These therapies can only deliver real results if the recipient commits to working on themselves after each session. If they commit to doing the homework they were given by the therapist in the area that they struggle with the most, genuine results can be seen.

In this book,**Pain-Free Easy Steps To a Happier Healthier You**, I look at how we have evolved our pain and escalated it to such a traumatic level, from the very beginning of our existence. What I offer is not a theory or myth, but an understanding of how we have come to burden ourselves with pain.

Pain is healthy. It's the body's natural indicator that something is not right within ourselves. Pain alerts us to take action and seek an immediate solution. When we start to heal, pain is part of the healing journey and lets us know that we are getting better.

Using up-to-date data from around the world and the latest medical research, I will show you how, in this self-help guide, you can retrain your thinking pattern, live in the 'now' and introduce new natural ways to nourish and move your body to eliminate pain. By doing this, you can begin to heal and greatly reduce or even eliminate unnecessary physical pain -possibly forever.

I will guide you through the pain journey, over each decade, using evidence and information from both the field of western and holistic medicine. You can then decide how you use the knowledge I have given you. To quote the Greek Philosopher Socrates : "Know thy self".

This book will allow you to do just that, to become closer to discovering the real you, and allow you to restore your own inner faith, revealing the new true you and healing years of unnecessary pain. When we let go of past emotional pain which no longer serves us, we start to live in a pain-free now. Surely that is all any person seeks?

1

IN THE BEGINNING
YOUR CREATION

"There are exactly as many special occasions in life as we choose to celebrate"
~ Robert Brault ~

The creation of man is the beginning of celebrating life. Taking time to celebrate often in your life helps remind you that it's worth being here. You don't have to pop a bottle of champagne every day, but you could if you felt like it. The point is to find something to celebrate each day. The more you celebrate and have the feeling of celebration, the more things will arrive in your life that you can celebrate.

If you save celebrations for a occasions, you will only have a few things a year to toast. This makes you feel that life is full of negative things not worth celebrating. Celebrating is like the ultimate form of thankfulness, and this is a powerful vibe to send out. Your birth was a time of celebration and each birthday you turn another year older is a time to honour who you are as a person, rather than, as some do, dreading what the future holds.

Birth of Medicine

History shows us we have used holistic medicine to heal our lives. As Socrates said in the 4th century B.C, "The part can never be well unless the whole is well".

Holistic health is a state of balance, not simply an absence of illness. Holistic health teaches the interconnection of mind, body, spirit and environment-just as it has for thousands of years. Long before penicillin or x-rays, healers recognised the importance of emotional and spiritual wellbeing in achieving physical health. Two of the most well-documented ancient holistic health traditions are Traditional Chinese Medicine (TCM) and Ayurveda.

TCM originated almost 5,000 years ago and has continued to evolve into a complex system of diagnostic and treatment methods that are still practised today. From the very beginning, TCM viewed the human body as a small universe of interconnected systems, including physical elements as well as subtle energies, such as "qi," or life force, and "shen" or spirit.

There are three ancient medical traditions in holistic health:

Ayurveda – Ayurveda is the ancient medical tradition of India. Ayurveda traces its origins to a text written by Sushruta, the "father of surgery" in the 6th century B.C. The healing practice incorporates beliefs in the five great elements of the universe, the seven primary constituent elements of the body, and the three "doshas," or biological energies, that each represents. Using a system of eight treatment disciplines, Ayurvedic holistic health practitioners guide their patients to balance and moderation.

Herbal Medicine – this emphasises holistic balance and is the oldest form of health care known to mankind. Indigenous people all over the world and throughout history have drawn on the medicinal properties of plants. Herbalism is a critical element of TCM and Ayurveda.

Western Herbalism – Western herbalism originated in ancient Greece and Rome, then spread throughout the rest of Europe and eventually to North and South America, focusing on the medicinal attributes of plants and herbs. Aromatherapy evolved from these foundations and the use of essential oils in healing the mind and body has found a dedicated place in helping towards healing stress.

Holistic Health Today

We live in a time of great imbalance. There are more pollutants and chemicals in our food and environment than ever before. We face epidemic rates of obesity and chronic disease. Most people have poor diet and exercise habits. Almost everyone in our fast-paced society struggles to manage daily stress, and one in every three people (including children) suffer from various degrees of chronic depression and anxiety, which are not always documented. There has never been a greater need for the holistic health approach. People are demanding medical alternatives and actively seeking better options for their personal wellness. This has resulted in constant research and development in the wellness industry.

Due to the great debate between medics and holistic therapists, as to whether the natural pathway works effectively, few medical doctors today practise holistic health care or make time to recommend it. This has seen an increase in more and more professionals being trained in holistic medicine to meet high demand. These holistic health practitioners use healing alternatives, such as massage therapy, nutrition, chiropractic medicine, acupuncture and homeopathic medicine to treat a variety of maladies. Whilst no holistic health practitioner or wellness professional can be an expert in every form of health restoration, each offers a unique toolbox of skills and knowledge to help patients achieve whole body health and balance.

Once we have restored a healthy state in the body, why don't we continue to heal through this approach? Why don't we integrate it as part of our daily/weekly/monthly routine for continued wellbeing? Why stop at just feeling good? Why not continue investing in yourself, working towards feeling amazing? By allowing ourselves regular therapy sessions, we can prevent illness from recurring or pain from getting worse.

Many ancient healing traditions are now enjoying renewed popularity. Newer healing modalities that were once dismissed are now being researched and respected. People are taking responsibility for their personal wellness and looking to trained professionals to help them on their path.

Successful holistic health practitioners are usually:

- Committed to lifelong learning
- Curious and open-minded
- Sensitive and compassionate
- A good listener and excellent verbal communicator
- Highly observant and detail-oriented
- Attentive to their own health and wellness

All these qualities I recognised in myself in my early twenties, which is why I chose a career as a holistic therapist. We look for these same traits in our doctors, consultants and nurses today, but struggle to find them. Whether due to heavy work pressure, government targets and long hours, they can no longer offer the time to give the patient what they seek, which a good professional therapist can.

Those fortunate enough to have a doctor who does take the time to really listen to their needs are the lucky ones. Most people have to wait up to three weeks to see a doctor, if it's not urgent, and after numerous tests and waiting months for a diagnosis, they're still no nearer to finding the answer to their persistent pain and problem.

It is therefore left in our own hands to look for the solution, if all other medical avenues have been closed. There is no wrong in seeking an alternate route to healing the mind and body. In fact, it's your natural gut instinct pre-programmed before birth that triggers you to search for it. Let's look how our pain journey began, from foetus to birth.

The Journey of Pain - Pre-birth

In 2006, the US federal government considered changing legislation to reduce abortion to 20 weeks to protect the unborn child, as growing evidence showed that the foetus experienced pain after 22 weeks. The National Right To Life Educational Trust Fund,

Washington DC Factsheet, suggests that all biological indicators in unborn children are capable of feeling pain by at least 20 weeks.

"At 20 weeks, the foetal brain has the full complement of brain cells present in adulthood, ready and waiting to receive pain signals from the body and their electrical activity can be recorded by standard electroencephalography (EEG)", confirms Dr Paul Ranalli, Neurologist, University of Toronto. Current UK legislation states, that abortion is legal in England, up to 24 weeks, under the Abortion Act of 1967.

Where there are those who strongly agree that the unborn child can feel pain, there are those who argue that the neural circuitry for pain in foetuses is immature and therefore has not yet developed, so the foetus will not understand that what it feels is actual pain.

Dr Stuart W.G. Derbyshire states, "To understand pain, you need to experience it and then the brain forms an understanding linking the two". The published paper by Dr Derbyshire, a senior lecturer at the University of Birmingham School of Psychology, on 15th April 2006 concludes that foetuses cannot feel pain.

Proof That the Foetus can Feel Pain

On 17th May 2012 Dr Colleen A. Malloy M.D, Assistant Professor in the Division of Neonatology Department of Paediatrics Northwestern University Feinberg School of Medicine, presented to the Committee of Judiciary in the U.S House of Representatives, scientific and clinical issues to support the pain pathway in the foetus. There is ample biologic, physiologic, hormonal and behavioural evidence for foetal and neonatal pain. In the Neonatal Intensive Care Unit, they witness first-hand the change of vital signs and even expressions on the foetus face which can be seen from 4D ultrasound imagery. When procedures such as IV placement or chest tube insertion are performed on neonates born at 20 weeks or more, the response is the same as in older infants and children. The foetus responds to sound by 20 weeks, as mothers will commonly report increased foetal movement in response to music, sirens or alarms. Dr Malloy concluded that the foetus and neonate born prior to term may have even heightened sensation of pain, compared to an infant more advanced in development.

In June 2015, the U.S House of Representatives passed the Bill 'Pain-Capable Unborn Child Protection Act' aimed at prohibiting doctors from performing abortions after 20 weeks of pregnancy, except in certain circumstances as set out in the Bill. The terms of the Bill are still being debated in Senate at time of publishing this book. My point is to show the strong evidence that currently exists that foetuses can feel physical pain and thus our pain pathway starts from the very beginning of our lives.

Proof That the Foetus can Hear

Published in the British Journal Ultrasound in October 2015, Dr Marisa López Teijón and Dr Álex Garcia-Faura, main authors of the clinical trial, presented at the press conference on the 6th October 2015, together with Professor Alberto Prats, Professor of Anatomy and Foetal Embryology at the Faculty of Medicine of the University of Barcelona, who also collaborated on the study.

Their study revealed that a 16-week-old foetus is already capable of hearing effectively and responding to music, as long as this is emitted from the mother's vagina. The foetuses respond to this stimulus with vocalisation movements, by opening their mouths and sticking out their tongues, which are previous to language acquisition.

A special device able to emit music from the vagina with an average intensity of 54 decibels (equivalent to a normal conversation), was designed for this study. The study proved that the unborn child as young as 16 weeks in development could hear and respond to sound. As the baby grows in the womb it continues to hear sound depth.

What the Unborn Child Hears - Sound

Sounds travel best through open space, you can hear someone shouting more easily in an open field than when your head is underwater in a pool, for instance. The foetus is surrounded by amniotic fluid and the amniotic sac, as well as layers of its mother's body. Sound will therefore be muffled, but heard. The louder a sound, the more likely the foetus can hear it. A barking dog, loud Hoover or wailing siren is going to sound more distinct than quiet background music.

The clearest noise the foetus will be able to hear is the mother. While most sound is transmitted through the air and then through the uterus, when a mother speaks, the sound of her voice reverberates through her bones and the rest of the body, amplifying it. Studies have shown that a foetus's heart rate increases when it hears the mother's voice, suggesting that the foetus becomes more alert when the mother speaks.

Babies also learn to recognise other voices and sounds, which they hear often in utero. Researchers from the Proceedings of the National Academy of Sciences (PNAS), have discovered that new-borns react differently to words and sounds that were repeated daily throughout the third term of pregnancy, compared to those they never heard during pregnancy. From inside the uterus, deeper, lower sounds are easier to establish than high-pitched sounds. So when the parent reads or sings to the foetus, it is learning their voice and responds accordingly.

Besides voice recognition, the foetus also feels the mother's emotional pathway, as it shares the mother's blood supply and hormone chemical release. When the mother is happy, she produces feel-good endorphins oxytocin, dopamine and serotonin. When she is stressed, she produces instantly the 'fight or flight' chemical adrenaline and 20 minutes later cortisol is released. The foetus will also absorb these. Too much adrenaline leads to a stressed unhappy baby, with a difficult birth.

What the Unborn Child can Feel – Emotions

A pregnant woman's thoughts have a physical connection to her unborn child. "Everything the pregnant mother feels and thinks is communicated through neurohormones to her unborn child, just as surely as are alcohol and nicotine," states Dr Thomas Verny.

As author of professional publications and founder of the Association for Prenatal and Perinatal Psychology and Health (APPPAH) and Journal of Prenatal and Perinatal Psychology and Health, Dr Verny is one of the world's leading authorities on the effects of prenatal environment on personality development.

What is an Emotion?

Medical dictionaries define emotion as a mental and physical state, referring to the hormones and other molecules associated with emotion. Deepak Chopra, M.D., further bridges the gap between the mental and physical state when he writes, "Thoughts that we feel are called emotions".

A pregnant woman's emotions are created based on the way she perceives her pregnancy, baby shower plans, nursery decoration, marriage, work and health. A pregnant woman's thoughts are the precursor for her emotions. And her emotions are the precursor for the neurohormones that Thomas Verny refers to.

In Magical Beginnings, Enchanted Lives, Dr Deepak Chopra clearly explains what pregnancy research is showing. "When a pregnant mother is anxious, stressed, or in a fearful state, the stress hormones released into her bloodstream cross through the placenta to the baby. Hundreds of studies have confirmed, that chemicals released by the pregnant mother's body are transported into the womb and affect the unborn baby".

Negative thoughts are often the root cause of a fear-based stress response. Deepak Chopra states, "Stress activates the unborn child's endocrine system and influences foetal brain development. Children born to mothers who had intensely stressful pregnancies are more likely to have behavioural problems later in life".

Thomas Verny says, "Studies show that mothers under extreme and constant stress are more likely to have babies who are premature, lower than average in weight, hyperactive, irritable, and colicky".

Cell biologist and neuroscientist Bruce Lipton, Ph.D. writes, "When passing through the placenta, the hormones of a mother experiencing chronic stress will profoundly alter the distribution of blood flow in her foetus and change the character of her developing child's physiology".

On the flip side Verny says, "Positive maternal emotions have been shown to advance the health of the unborn child". He continues, "Thoughts which infuse the developing baby with a sense of happiness or calm can set the stage for balance, happy and serene disposition throughout life".

Deepak Chopra agrees: "When you feel joyful, your body produces natural pleasure chemicals called endorphins and encephalins. When you are peaceful and relaxed, you release chemicals similar to prescription tranquillisers. Without stress, your baby's nervous system works smoothly. When you're calm and centred, your baby is able to grow peacefully".

The Power of Visualisation

In Nurturing the Unborn Child, Verny suggests 47 exercises that a pregnant woman can perform throughout pregnancy to support a stress-free baby and mother. One of these is creative visualisation. This form of mental imagery can programme one's subconscious thoughts, changing perceptions and responses from negative to positive, including physical behaviour.

Verny writes, "It has helped cure disease, enhance performance and improve state of mind. Used by ancient medicine men, shamans, and yogis for millennia, visualisation was long the first line of defence against disease".

Research has confirmed such imagery can alter blood flow, grow healthy cells and destroy cancer cells. Dr Lipton has even offered that a pregnant mother can affect her unborn child's genetic development. Whether it's called imagery, visualisation, meditation, or hypnosis, decades of research have established this process for generating a tangible changes in the mental, emotional and physical body.

I used visualisation from being a child. It was part of my imagination and creative ability to see things inside my head that others could not tap into. I first used visualisation successfully in my first pregnancy, during labour, when I had been over 30 hours in the process and getting nowhere. The stumbling block was my cervix which refused to dilate. It was just dormant.

The midwife encouraged me to visualise my cervix expanding by 1cm every 5 minutes until I became fully dilated to 10cms, which is when delivery of my newborn would take place. I decided that with every contraction I was having, which was every two minutes, I would close my eyes and imagine with great certainty, the space that needed to open was increasing with each big pain. Less than 15 minutes later, I told my husband to run and get the midwife back, as I was ready to push. She arrived rather flustered, as she had just made herself a cup of tea, thinking I wouldn't be ready to push, as I had only been 1cm dilated when she left. That was barely 15 minutes ago and I had been at 1cm for the past 16 hours without change. When she examined me, she became even more flustered, as she saw the baby's head crowning. My daughter was born six minutes later and thanks to visualisation, what seemed like an eternity of pain for me ended.

Birth

We've learnt that the unborn child can hear and feel the mother's emotional pathway as early as 16 weeks. If the mother continues to feel anxious, stressed, depressed or upset throughout her pregnancy, the baby will be born with stress and the delivery may be difficult. If, however, the mother is relaxed, happy, feeling blessed, and if she practises yoga, meditation and visualisation and talks lovingly to the baby, the birth point will be less shocking. The baby will be more placid and the birth will be easier.

It is well-known that psychological trauma of any sort can have a lasting, damaging effect on human beings. The earlier the trauma, the more profound the effect, so the impact of a difficult birth on the infant as it develops into a child and adult can be especially significant.

The Birth Experience

Imagine being a foetus. Imagine floating comfortably in the warm, soft, dark, fluid space of your mother's womb, drifting in and out of sleep, surrounded by muffled sounds and heartbeats. Then imagine the sudden shock of being awakened, and pushed and squeezed into the harsh, stark, and noisy outside world, amid your mother's pained shrieks, racing heart, and adrenaline- charged system.

Add to that the strain of an unusually long labour, painful forced delivery, or a life threatening situation, such as being strangled by the umbilical cord, and you have a major traumatic event. Then add the inevitable distress of the mother, to whom the baby is psychologically and energetically linked and you have a super trauma. Try to imagine, on top of all that, the added distress on the new-born infant of being removed from the mother for emergency treatment: the infant's or her own. What an incredibly cruel, loveless, unpredictable and scary place the world would seem to the distressed new born.

That is the experience and sensation that is imprinted onto the traumatised neonate's untainted mind. A newborn's immature nervous system is purely unconscious mind, combined with life or death driven emotion, so it does not have the cognitive capacity to be able to sort experiences and make sense of the world in a logical, conscious way. Its mind is like a blank sheet on which is printed the first experiences. And this imprint becomes the blueprint on which the child's life and future experiences are fashioned.

My younger sister Val, who has an extremely successful professional career, always felt like she was the 'unwanted child' and was born with the umbilical cord around her neck. She was the last of four pregnancies my mother had, the third a boy was miscarried at 26 weeks. My mother struggled with the last pregnancy (my sister), as she had to work right up to her birth without any time off, as money was exceptionally tight. I believe all my mother's stress and worry created a lot of turbulence inside the placenta and my sister did many somersaults due to the adrenaline and cortisol overload. Maybe this is why she now dislikes rollercoasters and fast rides and has a problem with vomiting!

My mother's high stress level during pregnancy contributed to the cord being wrapped around her neck so tight, that on delivery, it almost choked my sister. Although my sister's birth wasn't traumatic, it was enough to make her feel and become a sensitive and vulnerable individual, questioning many events in her life. In actual fact, without the cord round the baby's neck, it would have been the perfect birth - a smooth delivery after a very short labour, with no need for forceps or other aids.

Long Term Psychological Effects

Children who have had traumatic births are more likely to be anxious or aggressive than their easy-birth counterparts. Of course genetics and many other factors come into the equation too, but, if all else was equal, the child who was traumatised at birth would be more vulnerable to psychological problems. Separation from the mother at birth, as well as the mother's own post-trauma stress response, can affect the early bonding between the mother and child, which is another major factor in the child's psychological development. When treating clients in my clinic, the majority of adults confirm they suffered a difficult childhood. Most say they were a very quiet, withdrawn child, had difficulty making friends, were bullied by their peer group at school or just struggled in all areas with hyperactivity.

Rob was the last child born of six children, the baby of the family. His mother always said he was the easiest of them all. A really good pregnancy followed by a problem-free delivery, he was very much the wanted child. Yet Rob always carried a feeling of detachment, of never belonging. Rob recalls being a very placid little boy. As the youngest he was always spoken well of - until he turned 11.

He clearly remembers overhearing a conversation where his mum revealed that Rob was very much a wanted child. He had been specifically planned to replace his very sick brother, who was not expected to live after a severe accident. Rob was their insurance policy just in case his brother died. His brother didn't die, but this triggered the start of Rob's health issues and Obsessive Compulsive Disorder (OCD). This was also the beginning of his anxiety and depression, conditions he had carried within him, but never allowed to surface. At the time, he was not aware of it, but by the age of 17, he was officially diagnosed with it. Doctors confirmed it started as early as his adolescence, but his parents failed to accept it.

Rob struggled most of his adult life with failed relationships and his sexuality.

He found keeping a long-term job difficult and by the time he came to me, he had been off work for five years with health problems, both mentally and physically. He had long-term neck, shoulder and back problems. Doctors couldn't find anything physically wrong with him and he was left to his own devices to look for a cure. The back pain was preventing him from working.

We traced Rob's problems back to the age of 44 when his mother had suddenly passed away. He was extremely close to her even though he never felt truly loved by her. It was a difficult relationship, heightened because of his destructive father, who physically and mentally abused his children and wife, but Rob always adored his mum as he searched for a mother/child connection.

In 2012, at the age of 46, he made a decision to clean his lifestyle in order to ease his pain. He came off all his medication, started meditation, introduced drinking water daily and became a vegan. These changes made a huge difference, but he still had the pain he couldn't shift.

I met Rob for the first time at one of the leading Health and Complimentary Medicine Festivals in Ilkley, West Yorkshire. I was promoting my second book *Desperately Seeking A Pain-Free Self* and hosting a talk based on the treatment I founded, LT Therapy, and resetting muscle memory.

From the minute I started speaking, Rob was extremely attentive and after the talk he was one of the first people to grab my attention at the book signing. He completely related to everything I had explained, about how we hold onto emotional pain through the muscle memory system.

He booked an appointment at my Bradford clinic and I identified the continual pain he was feeling in the top right corner of his shoulder. This was where the brain deposits thoughts of his mother. His lower back represented his childhood and the root of who he was as a person. I clearly established that all his muscles where holding onto specific events in his life, which he was thinking about over and over again, but he couldn't change. He understood now why he was still feeling such discomfort.

Even if you change your physical routine, the brain is the computer that drives the body, so you need to also re-programme your thinking pattern or you continue to think in the same negative cycles, which created the physical pain.

For Rob, I reset each area using the LT Therapy method and told him to see me in a month. This would give him time to practise daily mind exercises, in order to help change his muscle memory pattern. If people struggle to do meditation or practise daily mindfulness and gratitude, I also recommend further support from a hypnotherapist who can help a person under hypnosis - with successful results.

At his review appointment, Rob's back was amazing. He not only had no recurring pain, but by practising daily mind exercises of meditation, mindfulness, gratitude and living in the 'now,' he had linked his mind to his physical pain. He had made the breakthrough and started to control his pain. He was now more relaxed and his anxiety and stress had gone, as he began to acknowledge his achievements and believe in himself.

He rebuilt the difficult relationship he had had with his adult son into a good solid happy one. Rob was always a very lovely, easy-going person, but like most of us, he allowed his negative patterns and past to haunt him. He now began to love, respect and value himself, rather than expecting it from others first. He felt confident to accept job opportunities that had begun flooding in and he began to laugh more, knowing that his journey in healing himself had always been in his own hands. Even when he had practised meditation in the past, it had been irregular and hence it hadn't allowed his mind to refocus on a new positive thinking pattern. By practising new skills daily, as Rob did, we can change the negative mindset into a positive one forever.

Rob isn't alone in his thinking. We've all been down that lost path of feeling detachment, rejected and unloved and suffering anxiety. It all stems from our pre-birth and early child hood years. In Chapter Two I'll look at this in more detail, but for now, understand that the relationship you had as the unborn child with your mother played a significant part in laying the foundations to who you become as an adult.

I know you had no control over it and we're not apportioning blame to the mother, for she alone cannot be fully accountable in how she carried you. Her circumstances, ignorance, health and her own perception of the pregnancy all play an important part.

Indeed, this might explain why some mothers have a stronger bond with their babies than others. This could also account for the pre and post-natal depression or 'baby blues' some woman suffer from. It's not all down to chemical changes and hormones. It can also be affected by the emotional state the mother was in at the time of conception. For example, was the baby planned, was the baby wanted, was it due to a one-night stand, was it accidental, was it conceived out of passion, necessity, duty or trauma?

Once the pregnancy is announced, the decisions that follow and the emotions the mother feels can mean either smooth sailing or a rollercoaster ride for the foetus. These questions will be debated till the end of our existence, but without a doubt, the formation of a human being is the greatest creation of all time and one that should be joyfully celebrated.

SUMMARY OF WHAT YOU HAVE LEARNED FROM THIS CHAPTER

- **Fact**: Holistic health is rapidly growing, due to high demand for a natural approach to wellbeing.

- **Fact**: The unborn child can hear sound from 16 weeks and feel pain at 20 weeks. By 24 weeks, the foetus can feel the mother's emotional pathway.

- **Fact**: Stressed mothers can have difficult pregnancies and births, which in turn can cause the child to become problematic in the early years.

- **Fact**: How we are born and our circumstance has a direct effect on our emotions, which can lead to pain developing over our lifetime.

WHAT YOU CAN DO RIGHT NOW TO CHANGE THINGS FOR THE BETTER

- Today, one of the many popular pastimes for many people is searching their ancestry, as they seek a sense of belonging and connection. Understanding how you came into the world will help you identify how your pain journey began, if it was as far back as your birth or primary years. Looking back in this way is healthy for those who wish to truly get to the root of their pain and a deeper realisation of who they really are as a person. Also, this allows you to create a better appreciation of your parent or parents, no matter how difficult the start of the journey was. They too had a hard time working out how to be a parent, taking responsibility without any training.

- Reflecting on difficult past events and acknowledging them in a positive way means you take responsibility for yourself and you don't apportion blame. Feeling negative and blaming others only builds negative cells that are like large storage tanks. These tanks keep filling with unhappy events that you can access anytime in your life. Every time you recall such a negative memory, you are recycling the event, releasing chemicals in your body that only lead to pain. Replace any negative emotions with love and forgiveness. If this exercise is too difficult to do on your own, share it with someone you can trust, who can support you, or a therapist or professional, such as a trained psychologist. By turning how you see your past from a negative to a positive, you will start to train your brain in a healthy way, which in turn allows your body to naturally heal, restoring physical wellbeing.

2

THE PRIMARY YEARS

BIRTH TO AGE 10

"Children must be taught how to think not what to think"

~ Margaret Mead ~

From the minute we are born, we learn. It is therefore critical that our care in the early years is a loving, trusting, secure environment, in order to develop our experience both emotionally and physically in a positive state. A child's relationship with a consistent, caring adult in the early years is associated with healthier behaviours, more positive peer interactions, increased ability to cope with stress, and better school performance later in life. Babies who receive affection and nurturing from their parents have the best chance of healthy development. Warm, sensitive and responsive parenting promotes feelings of safety and security within the child, providing children with the confidence to explore and engage with their surroundings.

Children learn to trust that their parents will be there for them when they need something, when they are hurt, or when they have encountered something upsetting. Parental warmth - touching, holding, comforting, rocking, singing and talking calmly - can help children manage their emotional experience. This can contribute to the reduction of behaviour problems in the later years.

So how does the link between our relationship with our parents in the early years affect both our physical and emotional pain later in life? It has a huge impact. The lack of a nurturing environment leads to emotional detachment between child and parent, which influences the child's development throughout their life. This special connection is called The Attachment Bond.

Have you ever been in love? We all have, at least once. The attachment bond is the term for our first interactive love relationship, the one you had with your primary caregiver as an infant, usually your mother. This mother-child attachment bond shapes an infant's brain, profoundly influencing their self-esteem, expectations of others and their ability to attract and maintain successful adult relationships.

By learning about attachment, you can build healthier, attuned relationships, and communicate more effectively, subsequently reducing and even eliminating pain. John Bowlby was a British psychologist, psychiatrist and psychoanalyst, notable for his interest in child development and for his pioneering work in attachment theory. His work, Review of General Psychology survey, published in 2002, ranked Bowlby as the 49th most cited psychologist of the 20th century.

Attachment, Bonding and Relationships

Bowlby's theory is that we were born preprogrammed to bond with one very significant person, our primary caregiver, probably our mother. Like all infants, we were a bundle of emotions intensely experiencing fear, anger, sadness and joy. The emotional attachment that grew between you and your caregiver was the first interactive relationship of your life, and it depended upon nonverbal communication. The bonding you experienced determined how you would relate to other people throughout your life, because it established the foundation for all verbal and nonverbal communication in your future relationships.

Individuals who experience confusing, frightening or broken emotional communications during their infancy often grow into adults who have difficulty understanding their own emotions and the feelings of others. This limits their ability to build or maintain successful relationships. Attachment—the relation-ship between infants and their primary caregivers—is responsible for:

- shaping the success or failure of future intimate relationships
- the ability to maintain emotional balance
- the ability to enjoy being ourselves and to find satisfaction in being with others
- the ability to rebound from disappointment, discouragement and misfortune

Scientific study of the brain and the role attachment plays in shaping it has given us a new basis for understanding why vast numbers of people have great difficulty communicating with the most important individuals in their work and love lives. Once, we could only use guesswork to try and determine why important relationships never evolved, developed chronic problems or fell apart. Now, thanks to new insights into brain development, we can understand what it takes to help build and nurture productive and meaningful relationships at home and at work.

What is the Attachment Bond?

The mother-child bond is the primary force in infant development, according to the Attachment Bond Theory, pioneered by English psychiatrist John Bowlby and American psychologist Mary Ainsworth. The theory has gained strength through worldwide scientific studies and the use of brain imaging technology.

The attachment bond theory states that the relationship between infants and primary caretakers is responsible for:

- shaping all of our future relationships
- strengthening or damaging our abilities to focus, be conscious of our feelings, and calm ourselves
- the ability to bounce back from misfortune

Research reveals the infant/adult interactions that result in a successful, secure attachment are those where both mother and infant can sense the other's feelings and emotions. In other words, an infant feels safe and understood when the mother responds to their cries and accurately interprets their changing needs. Unsuccessful or insecure attachment occurs when there is a failure in this communication of feelings.

Researchers found that successful adult relationships depend on the ability to:

- manage stress
- stay "tuned in" with emotions
- use communicative body language
- be playful in a mutually engaging manner
- be readily forgiving, relinquishing grudges

The same research also found that an insecure attachment may be caused by abuse, but it is just as likely to be caused by isolation or loneliness. These discoveries offer a new glimpse into successful love relationships, providing the keys to identifying and repairing a love relationship that is on the rocks. It is also this same connection that connects to our pain pathway. When you are stressed, anxious, sad, afraid or upset, you produce adrenaline and cortisol. This doesn't just happen to adults - infants produce it at the same level. This accumulation of adrenaline - our 'fight or flight' response – is stored as lactic acid if it's unused, and it leads to acute and chronic pain.

The Attachment Bond - How it Shapes an Infant's Brain

The infant brain is profoundly influenced by the attachment bond, a baby's first love relationship. When the primary caretaker can manage personal stress, calm the infant, communicate through emotion, share joy and forgive easily, the young child's nervous system becomes "securely attached". The strong foundation of a secure attachment bond enables the child to be self-confident, trusting, hopeful and comfortable in the face of conflict. As an adult, he or she will be flexible, creative, hopeful and optimistic.

Our secure attachment bond shapes our abilities to:

- feel safe
- develop meaningful connections with others
- explore our world
- deal with stress
- balance emotions
- experience comfort and security
- make sense of our lives
- create positive memories and expectations of relationships

Attachment Bonds are as unique as we are. Primary caretakers don't have to be perfect. They do not have to always be in tune with their infants' emotions, but it helps if they are emotionally available the majority of the time.

Insecure Attachment Affects Adult Relationships

Insecurity can be a significant problem in our lives, and it takes root when an infant's attachment bond fails to provide the child with sufficient structure, re-cognition, understanding, safety and mutual accord. These insecurities may lead us to:

- **Tune Out and Turn Off** – If our parent is unavailable and self-absorbed, we may as children get lost in our own inner world, avoiding any close, emotional connections. As adults, we may become physically and emotionally distant in relationships.
- **Remain Insecure** – If we have a parent who is inconsistent or intrusive, it's likely we will become anxious and fearful, never knowing what to expect. As adults, we may be available one moment and rejecting the next.
- **Become Disorganised, Aggressive and Angry** – When our early needs for emotional closeness go unfulfilled, or when a parent's behaviour is a source of disorientation or terror, problems are sure to follow. As adults, we may not love easily and may be insensitive to the needs of our partner.
- **Develop Slowly** – Such delays manifest themselves as deficits and result in subsequent physical and mental health problems, and social and learning disabilities. This could

be one reason why we are now seeing a sudden spurt in undiagnosed conditions such as ADD and ADHD, in both children as well as adults.

TABLE TO ILLUSTRATE THE ATTACHMENT THEORY IN HUMAN BEHAVIOUR

Attachment Style	Parental Style	Resulting Adult Characteristics
SECURE	Aligned with the child; in tune with the child's emotions	Able to create meaningful relationships; empathetic; able to set appropriate boundaries
AVOIDANT	Unavailable or rejecting	Avoids closeness or emotional connection; distant; critical; rigid; intolerant
INDECISIVE	Inconsistent and sometimes intrusive parent communication	Anxious and insecure; controlling; blaming; erratic; unpredictable; sometimes charming
DISORGANISED	Ignored or didn't see child's needs; parental behaviour was frightening/ traumatizing	Chaotic; insensitive; explosive; abusive; untrusting even while craving security
REACTIVE	Extremely unattached or malfunctioning	Cannot establish positive relationships; often misdiagnosed

Varying parental styles and types of attachment bonds are found throughout any population, culture, ethnic or socio-economic group.

Causes of Insecure Attachment

Major causes that contribute to insecure attachments include:

- **physical neglect** – poor nutrition, insufficient exercise and neglect of medical issues
- **emotional neglect or emotional abuse** – little attention paid to child, little or no effort to understand child's feelings; verbal abuse
- **physical or sexual abuse** – physical injury or violation
- **separation from primary caregiver** – due to illness, death, divorce, adoption
- **inconsistency in primary caregiver** – succession of nannies or staff at private nurseries.
- **frequent moves or placements** – constantly changing environment; for example: children who spend their early years in orphanages or who move from foster home to foster home
- **traumatic experiences** – serious illnesses or accidents
- **maternal depression** – withdrawal from maternal role due to isolation, lack of social support, hormonal problems
- **maternal addiction to alcohol or other drugs** – maternal responsiveness reduced by mind-altering substances
- **young or inexperienced mother** – lacks parenting skills

The lessons of Understanding 'Attachment' Help us Heal Ourselves and our Adult Relationships

The powerful life-altering lessons we learn from our attachment bond, our first love relationship with our caregiver, continues to teach us as adults. The gut level knowledge we gained then guides us in improving our adult relationships and making them secure. Remember, that our gut is driven by the unconscious mind, where our inner child lives and is the true essence of who we are.

Adult relationships depend for their success on nonverbal forms of communication. Infants cannot talk, reason or plan, yet they are equipped to make sure their needs are met. Infants don't know what they need. They feel what they need, and communicate accordingly. When an infant communicates with their carer who understands and meets their physical and emotional needs, something wonderful occurs.

Relationships in which the parties are tuned in to each other's emotions are called attuned relationships, and attuned relationships teach us that:

- nonverbal cues deeply impact our love relationships
- play helps us smooth over the rough spots in love relationships
- conflicts can build trust if we approach them without fear or a need to punish

When we can recognise that past painful memories, expectations, attitudes, assumptions and behaviours, resulting from insecure attachment bonds established in childhood, we can end their influence on our negative adult behaviour and heal our physical and emotional pain. That recognition allows us to reconstruct the healthy nonverbal communication skills that produce an attuned attachment and successful individual in relationships.

Using this theory as part of our foundation to pain, you can slowly start to look at your own childhood and see how it influenced your life and primarily your wellbeing. This is not about apportioning blame, whether you were starved of love and emotional connection due to poor parenting; it is to develop a deeper and clearer understanding of how your unexplained pain got to where it is now. It is also the journey of discovering how it triggered illnesses and difficult relationships along the way.

I would say that 95% of the clients I treat and have treated had difficulties in their primary years, (from birth to aged 10) - even those who believed they had a good childhood and great parents still struggled with aspects of belonging.

If we look back within the last hundred years and see how parents raised their children, a whole collection of variable pressures from their place in society, wealth, home, work and friends would determine whether the child had a good start in life or carried the stress of their parents' worries. The developing brains of infants and toddlers are wired to expect responsive, warm, and sensitive interactions with parents and caregivers. But if that doesn't happen, children can suffer. Children in families experiencing hardship or poverty often witness stress, in the form of sadness and anger, from their parents and don't get the nurturing they need. This can affect children's abilities to understand and read people's emotions. Children as young as two can also experience sleep disturbances, become withdrawn, or display aggressive behaviours. Toilet training becomes delayed and bed wetting can continue into the early school years. These and other negative behaviours can follow them into later childhood and adulthood.

Some people have been seen by every doctor and consultant, and have had numerous tests, scans and x-rays and are still no closer to finding the real cause of their ongoing pain. They're caught in a loop, like a record played on repeat, seeking any solutions that could help put an end to it.

Through research and writing, I've learned that my own pain didn't commence in childhood, one that was filled with emotional and physical pain. It started long before I was born. Hardship fell on my parents' shoulders, after they lost their identities through extreme events in their childhood, causing them to flee their own countries. Two innocent and hopeful immigrants, searching for a better life in England, brought with them only a small suitcase of clothes, which reflected all their worldly possessions. At the time, they were not aware that they were also carrying with them a history of disappointment, fear, anger and suffering that would be reflected in how they would manage their family and their future.

Our First Decade on Planet Earth

It's extremely important to understand that your childhood holds the key to your pain. We can establish this due to the Attachment Theory. Once you accept this understanding, you can then see how the relationships you formed with those around pre-school leads to your behaviour when you finally start.

Can you remember your first day at school and how comfortable or uncomfortable you felt? Did you cry as soon as you were left or did you join in to the new environment and form friendships straight away? I remember feeling so lost, empty and abandoned; for sure I cried.

I now understand why it felt so deep for me. A year earlier before starting school, at the age of four, my brother and I had contracted gastroenteritis from one of my mum's friend's children. In 1967 children who had such an aggressive form of this illness were hospitalised and placed in individual isolation rooms. I remember my poor mother was refused any direct contact with us, in case she carried the virus or bacteria back out to others. We both stayed in separate areas of the hospital for a whole month, with no direct contact allowed, being tube-fed initially and then later when things stabilised, fed by a nurse. I remember staying in my cot, clinging on to the rails, constantly crying, as I desperately reached out for my mother. All that separated me from her was a pane of glass.

This, my prison, was one of the reasons that caused me to feel emotions of rejection, neglect, being deserted, unwanted and empty. These negative memories connect to my unconscious mind, forming how I would begin to perceive the outside world. This now starts to form part of my personality and how I will approach people later in adult life. How many of us hide behind a staged front - acting confident, self-assured, strong and in control? Most of us mask our emotions to protect ourselves from getting hurt and feeling pain.

Challenging childhoods dominated by bullying, feeling unloved, deprivation and abuse activate our 'survival' mode. This button lies dormant in all of us. It goes 'live' when we recognise later in life the same emotions we created in our primary years. These emotions resurface when triggered by different events, but we react the same way, because we do it instinctively.

This is easily demonstrated in the school playground. Say you are playing at the usual break time and want to join in the trendy game everyone in your peer group (tribe) are playing. There is always a leader who decides who can and cannot join in - usually that person is little Miss or Mr Popular. This happened to me every day at primary school and I was rejected by my peers, due to my foreign name or not wearing 'cool' clothes. I was left to my own devices, playing on my own.

This allowed me to channel my creative side, but at the same time added to my low self-esteem. I would play with my whip and top. For those too young to remember, a whip and top was a small leather whip on a wooden stick and a wooden cone, the size of a pine cone. You would wrap the leather whip part around the cone and then release it quickly, sending the cone in a spin on the ground. By whipping it fast, you kept it spinning, adding to the fun of the game.

I was so good at that game that I drew a crowd. Nobody could beat me at how long I could keep it spinning. I won a few friends from it, mainly those from the African Caribbean crowd. They said I had a lot of rhythm, I was a natural, which also made me great at the hula hoop, another game you can play on your own or with others.

As you grow older, you see the same people who were once the original popular kids in the playground, who always got to control who joined in or not, do the same thing as adults in their workplace. They take the same control in their relationships and with their family. People who never fully grow up become manipulative. Those who do grow are the ones who genuinely are self-assured, care for others, attain their goals and succeed in all areas of their lives.

Those who live in their inner child, who allow their negative past from their primary years to dominate, become adults who fail to achieve successful meaningful relationships with partners, family and work colleagues. They struggle to complete personal goals and blame everything around them and other people for their failure in achieving things in life.

Our Behaviour Can Unite or Divide

Just before this book went to publication, the UK made a historic decision on 23rd June 2016. It voted to come out of the European Union (EU). It sent shock waves around the world that the people of Great Britain had decided to take back their country and establish independence. Like any long-term marriage, the warning signs were there - you stop listening, there's an obvious breakdown in communication and suddenly a division starts to form.

You love your partner, but are no longer 'in love' with them, so the only solution is to seek a divorce. This is how many people viewed our relationship with the EU. What shocked me personally was the public outcry and behaviour on social media. People sent abusive and antagonistic remarks to those in the opposite camp. People who would not say boo to a ghost suddenly posted hostile comments. One lady even blamed the result for triggering her depression.

This uneasy response was escalated right up the ranks to those in Parliament, where the division continued. We live today in a democracy, where everyone has the right to an opinion and everyone's decision, no matter what, should be respected. No one can tell how something difficult to accept will turn out in the long run, but this is not a time to apportion blame. It's a time to come together, united as a team, working to our strengths. By attacking the situation with negative thinking, it triggers a platform for more hostility, unrest and detachment. Fear is what drives people to this negative approach – it is fear of the unknown, as most people don't embrace change well and will effectively create unnecessary mental and physical pain.

Britain felt that same fear on the brink of World War Two. The government's motivational poster campaign of 1939 stated, 'Keep Calm and Carry on.' This motto saved the British people from annihilation by its European counterparts, by bringing a nation to work together, strengthening our roots, making it a victorious Great Britain.

SUMMARY OF WHAT YOU HAVE LEARNED FROM THIS CHAPTER

- **Fact**: Attachment and bonding with your caregiver from the minute you are born is crucial to good emotional development.

- **Fact**: It shapes the success or failure of your intimate relationships, maintains emotional balance and helps you manage stress.

WHAT YOU CAN DO RIGHT NOW TO CHANGE THINGS FOR THE BETTER

- Look back at your earlier years in a positive way. If there is a challenging event, time or person that you keep visiting back in your memory, focus on seeing how strong the experience made you. Engage the help of a professional therapist as your support, if it becomes too difficult to review these memories on your own.

- Remember the past does not equal your present and it no longer is a memory that serves to help you. It is also something you cannot change. Thinking about it only serves to harm you. Recognise this and transform that thinking pattern into letting it go. In your mind fill a balloon with the memory. Tie a knot to seal it, then release the balloon. See it floating high above you in the sky climbing higher and higher until it disappears. It's gone!

3

THE SECONDARY YEARS

10 TO 20, BECOMING A YOUNG ADULT

"Be so good they can't ignore you"

~ Steve Martin ~

Here's a way to assure yourself of success. Just be so good that you can't be ignored. This can work in your personal and professional life, no matter what you're doing. You can do it so well that you are a standout and a force to be reckoned with. If you apply this quote to even the most mundane tasks you face, you'll find that you have a new zest for doing it better. You will keep your partner interested in you, keep your boss happy with your work and keep your customers happy with your product or service.

If we all started our teenage life with this motivational thought in mind, I wonder how many would feel a whole lot better about themselves. In the USA, they encourage their young generations of teens to be the best they can in schools and at home. They listen to this mantra of success every day. Soon they begin to believe it; hence the U.S produces some of the best world class athletes, sport players, musicians, entertainers, inventors and entrepreneurs of our time.

Pain in this decade would be overridden if we accepted changes more readily, rather than cowering from it - which leads us to ask, how does pain continue to grow in our teens? These are the transitional years, when we move from dependency to becoming independent. In a recent study, when I asked my clients which decade was their most difficult emotionally, they cited age 10 to 20 or 15 to 25. Ironically this is the period when our brain is still developing. Latest figures taken from The Samaritans Statistics Report 2015 show that one of the highest suicide rates is amongst males aged 15 to 19, closely followed by females.

These turbulent years reflect our most challenging period of emotional pain, as we battle to fit in with our peers, graduate from primary to secondary school, juggle uncontrollable hormones, discover our sexuality, continue to please our parents or deal with loss, separation and divorce. For some, the first decade was a rough ride, but things just got a whole lot worse. For those who had an enchanted start, you will learn coping techniques as you are challenged later in life. Even changing from primary to senior school comes as a great shock, as you leave a comfortable, protected, safe setting and enter the lion's den. But the whole point of being on this planet is to learn about ourselves and learning through responsibility, value, change, rejection and pain is all part of that journey.

We don't know all this at the time, as we are just becoming young adults; the world is a big adventure and most of us have no map or compass to guide us through these unstable years. Your map and compass should have been your parents, but if they never had these tools in their childhood, how can they pass them on to you? Now more than any other time, the connection we have with our parents and the bond we made is crucial for how we respond to our new environment. It will shape our decisions for the future and affect our behaviour with authority, but most of all, it will remain in our unchartered unconscious mind, lying dormant until our later years, where it will emerge as both physical and emotional pain.

I clearly remember leaving primary school where I was alienated, hoping the next school, which was a middle school, would be better. But the bullying continued. I was there from 11 to 13, when I was in the early stages of changing and developing; new parts of my body were emerging. I was becoming a young woman and didn't like the attention it brought. My low self-esteem made me compare myself to all the other girls in my class and how I had everything going so wrong for me. Acne sprouted like marigolds re-seeding. When I got rid of one group, another outbreak started.

I had NHS prescription glasses at the age of 12 – I'd struggled to read the blackboard (known as whiteboard today), which only added to the intimidation. Being made to sit at the front of the class only made me more of a target, and I became known as 'clever clogs', 'know it all' or the 'teacher's pet.' The glasses had done me no favours.

Fast forward in today's society, glasses are seen (no pun intended) as the 'in' accessory; people who don't even need glasses are wearing them as a fashion statement. How times have changed.

There is something nice about being pure and innocent in a volatile realm. I felt like I'd been thrown into the gladiator's arena without any weapons. It's then that you quickly learn how to protect, defend and survive. Even though I was doing this at home, I couldn't seem to do it amongst my peers. They were on my level, but seemed more threatening than my father. He was very violent for no reason. He took his difficulties out on his blameless family - me, my brother, sister and mother. I suppose I knew where I stood with him as a battering piece, but with my peers who were my equals, I did not.

Walking to school, I felt I was escaping from the shouting and hostility at home, but arriving at school, I moved from the war zone to stealth manipulation. I moved from class to class, trying to blend in, trying to be invisible, closing my ears to ridicule, hoping not to be directly attacked. The classroom was my hiding place, no one could torment me there, the teacher was my defender and if anyone did anything out of line, they would be punished immediately. At break time, I would find a quiet corner to eat my lunch, or hope the library was open, so I could hide and read more books. I loved the silence there, as I never knew it at home, unless my father went out.

These are the years that created most of my pain emotionally, as I now understood more about how brutal and hard life was becoming. I struggled to identify which direction I needed to go in, in order to find my true self. One thing I did know, was that I wanted a strong education; with that came knowledge and knowledge brought power, freedom and security, all elements I was starved of.

Unfortunately, my father always called me stupid, which again only added to the decline of my belief system. He never believed in higher education for women. I was never going to be financially supported, so I had to reject my place at Oxford Polytechnic to do business and language studies. Instead, I ventured into the working world at 18, with my father's seal of approval, but inside, I felt a part of me had died. My door to education had closed. Fate, however, would offer me another window to open in years to come, but at the time, I didn't know that.

I was always vigilant and quite mature for my years. When I moved to my final school, from age 13 to 18, I was known as the 'problem solver', the 'agony aunt' and the 'Marjorie Proops'. I even had the glasses! The bullying had stopped and the bitching had begun. I was in the right place to experience it, a Roman Catholic all-girls school. It was 1977 and education was changing. My school had moved from being private to now being state-run. I was the first of the new breed of non-paying pupils at the school, privately run by nuns. The existing students - still wearing straw hats as I started in the September term – looked upon me as vermin. Even though money was tight, my mother ensured I would be dressed impeccably and I did look fab in my blue and red posh attire - only the accessories of acne and spectacles pulled me down.

I did find a small group of girls I could relate to; they became my tribe. They were, like me, of foreign descent. Their families were immigrants merging from Eastern and Western countries, who came to England in the late 1950s for work and a new life. A mixture of Polish, Ukraine, Hungarian, Latvian and Italian, these girls all had secrets about home , just like me. I could keep any secret, which is probably why I'm such a good therapist today, never breaking a trust, adhering to the strict code of client confidentiality. I couldn't talk then about my own life at home, in case it caused trouble and I knew what the consequences of that would be. I had developed great empathy and a deep understanding when it came to listening to other people's problems, always deflecting mine, too scared to share for fear of repercussions. The girls couldn't figure out how I had attained such wisdom at such a young age. My name Sophia means wisdom! Thanks to my difficult primary years at home and at school, with the added bonus from the bullying years in my middle school, I was ahead of my peers when it came down to affairs of the heart.

These were the years you needed your wits about you, as you started to prepare for your exams, GCSEs and A levels. But most of my friends were nursing broken hearts over pop stars, icons they saw as rock gods – all part of becoming attracted to the opposite sex. Unfortunately, the school opposite just happened to be a Roman Catholic all-boys school, which had changed its education status at the same time. Girls got crushes on teachers and envisaged marriage with children in their Biology lessons. Hormones escalated, as quickly as their skirts shortened, when any male walked past, breaking school law. Make-up was sneaked in, crushing another forbidden rule, but girls couldn't live without mascara and eyeliner, as they secretly had liaisons with boys from the opposite school during their lunch break. My dearest friend Carol used to meet her boyfriend most lunchtimes at the school gates and couldn't see him without her 'eyes on.' For me, that would mean my glasses; for her it was her mascara and eyeliner.

Instead of retaining knowledge for algebra, the structure of English grammar and formulas, the only chemistry the girls were interested in was nowhere to be found in a science lab. Did I ever have time to feel like this, time to dream, time to fantasise? Yes of course I did, but never with a real person. I was too busy buried in my books and had learned from my friends that boys break your heart which leads to emotional pain. I had had enough emotional pain at home, so I didn't really want any more outside. Instead,

I just enjoyed the best my imagination could give me - Starsky & Hutch, Donny Osmond and John Travolta never gave me such grief. I could create any scenario I wanted and they would never let me down.

Why do we create escapism at a time when we need to focus? Is this where we begin to learn the skill of procrastination? The moment our mind doesn't want to grow up and take responsibility, when we still want to play like children? Is this a way our mind protects our body from pain? Scientists have traditionally thought that a person's brain growth was complete and the structure was more or less fixed by the age of three. They believed that connections between neurons were rewired as children went off to school and acquired information; scientists confirmed then that the blueprint for the brain was set.

Today with modern science and new discoveries, we see that the brain is not fully developed until our early twenties. Could this hold the key as to why teenagers in the second decade of their life suffer so much stress leading to suicides, alcohol/drug abuse and mixed sexuality? Did those people who were once teenagers decades ago feel the same, but, due to a lack of understanding, suffered in silence?

This type of hurt is disguised as self-harm. When we suffer with anxiety and depression, we are lost amongst our peers, suffocated under a society who hide from the truth and shelter any form of healing.

The Adolescent Brain Under Construction

In their search for the causes of mental illness scientists have studied the development of the brain from birth to adulthood. Powerful new technologies have enabled them to track the growth of the brain and to investigate the connections between brain function, development and behaviour. The research has turned up some surprises, including the discovery of striking changes taking place during the teen years. These findings have altered long-held assumptions about the timing of brain maturation.

The brain doesn't look like that of an adult until the early 20s. An understanding of how the brain of an adolescent is changing may help explain the contradiction of adolescence. Young people at this age are close to a lifelong peak of physical health, strength and mental capacity, and yet, for some, this can be a hazardous age. Mortality rates jump between early and late adolescence. Rates of death by injury between ages 15 to 19 are about six times that of the rate between ages 10 and 14. Crime rates are highest among young males and rates of alcohol abuse are high, relative to other ages.

Even though most adolescents come through this transitional age, the risk factors can have serious consequences. Genes, childhood experience and the environment in which a young person reaches adolescence all shape behaviour. Adding to this complex picture, research is revealing the brain is still changing, and that has its own impact on behaviour.

The more we learn, the better we may be able to understand the abilities and vulnerabilities of teens, and the significance of this stage, for life-long mental and physical health. The fact that so much change is taking place beneath the surface may be something for parents to keep in mind during the ups and downs of adolescence.

The Brain

A clue to the degree of change taking place in the teen brain came from studies in which scientists did brain scans of children as they grew from early childhood through to the age of 20. The scans revealed unexpectedly late changes in the volume of grey matter, which forms the thin, folding outer layer or cortex of the brain. The cortex is where the processes of thought and memory are based. Over the course of childhood, the volume of grey matter in the cortex increases and then declines. A decline in volume is normal at this age and is in fact a necessary part of growth.

The assumption for many years had been that the volume of grey matter was highest in very early childhood, and gradually fell as a child grew. The more recent scans, however, revealed that the high point of the volume of grey matter occurs during early adolescence. While the details behind the changes in volume on scans are not completely clear, the results push the timeline of brain development into adolescence and young adulthood. In terms of the volume of grey matter seen in brain images, the brain does not begin to resemble that of an adult until the early 20s. The scans also suggest that different parts of the cortex mature at different rates. Areas involved in more basic functions mature first: those involved, for example, in the processing of information from the senses and in controlling movement. The parts of the brain responsible for controlling impulses and planning ahead, the hallmarks of adult behaviour, are among the last to mature.

A Spectrum of Change

Research from the National Institute of Mental Health (NIH) are using many different approaches, showing that more than grey matter is changing:

- Connections between different parts of the brain increase throughout childhood and well into adulthood. As the brain develops, the fibres connecting nerve cells are wrapped in a protein that greatly increases the speed with which they can transmit impulses from cell to cell. This increase in connectivity, a little like providing a growing city with a fast, integrated communication system, shapes how well different parts of the brain work in tandem. Research is finding that the extent of connectivity is related to growth in intellectual capacities, such as memory and reading ability.
- Several lines of evidence suggest that the brain circuitry involved in emotional responses is changing during the teen years. Functional brain imaging studies, for example, suggest that the responses of teens to emotionally loaded images and situations are heightened relative to younger children and adults. The brain changes underlying these patterns involve brain centres and signalling molecules that are part of the reward system with which the brain motivates behaviour.

These age-related changes shape how much different parts of the brain are activated in response to experience and in terms of behaviour, the urgency and intensity of emotional reactions.

- Enormous hormonal changes take place during adolescence. Reproductive hormones shape not only sex-related growth and behaviour, but overall social behaviour. Hormone systems involved in the brain's response to stress are also changing during the teens. As with reproductive hormones, stress hormones can have complex effects on the brain, and as a result, behaviour.

- In terms of sheer intellectual power, the brain of an adolescent is a match for an adult's. The capacity of a person to learn will never be greater than during adolescence. At the same time, behavioural tests, sometimes combined with functional brain imaging, suggest differences in how adolescents and adults carry out mental tasks. Adolescents and adults seem to engage different parts of the brain to different extents, during tests requiring calculation and impulse control, or in reaction to emotional content. This may explain why teens are so good at computer gaming!

- Research suggests that adolescence brings with it brain-based changes in the regulation of sleep that may contribute to teens' tendency to stay up late at night. Along with the obvious effects of sleep deprivation, such as fatigue and difficulty maintaining attention, inadequate sleep is a powerful contributor to irritability and depression. Studies of children and adolescents have found that sleep deprivation can increase impulsive behaviour; some researchers report finding that it is a factor in delinquency. Adequate sleep is central to physical and emotional health.

Teen Pressure

No matter what decade you lived in as a teenager, it had its own pressures. If you are reading this book as a mature adult, you are doing so to hopefully find the reason behind your existing pain today. At the same time, if you have children or grandchildren, whether young or old, you can help identify their pain too. Seeking a solution to why you suffer so much pain will help you identify the root cause and with that information, you can begin to heal by working on yourself, using proven self-help techniques, that succeed at any age. You can also incorporate professional support.

Pain is a tool which you were given at birth. Besides being there to recognise when you need medical help, it's there when you need emotional support too. Most of us allow it to get to such a bad state, staying in denial rather than admit something is not right. Only after much hurt do we take the necessary action.

Which decade living as a teen was the worst? Don't all shout out at once and say, 'Mine was!' Of course it was, you were actually there, unless it was the 60's. They say if you remember the 60s, you never were there! If you had a tail spin of pressure then, today's complex world has thrown the next generation of teenagers into a tornado of such great magnitude, they are struggling to make their mark.

Social media is responsible for so much of today's teen image problems of stick thin celebrities, which lead to eating disorders, cyber bullying, self-harm, suicide and suicide attempts. Endless selfie pictures, with a dramatic need to show washboard stomachs and Barbie doll features, adorn Facebook, Twitter, Instagram and Snapchat, to name a few.

Meeting Parent Expectations

The introduction of pressure began in our primary years, but most of us did not understand it. It becomes more evident in the secondary years, when we are expected to live up to other people's expectations of us. For most of us, if you had parents, they wanted you to do well for two reasons. First, so they can look at you and see that you have achieved the same or more than they did, which means on reflection, they have succeeded in being a good parent. Secondly, so they can brag or boast about you to their friends and neighbours. Again, this is a reflection of their great parenting, as you indirectly represent them.

People create 'trophy' kids. You see this more and more in today's society and on social media. Parents live out their dreams through their children's success. They push their children to succeed, where they once failed. Again, you can look at this in two different ways. First parents see themselves in you, as you are genetically a part of who they are. If they failed in any part of their life, they don't want to see the same happen to you, so as a protection, they push you to succeed.

Secondly, where you succeed, they succeed in living the dream. By the way, whilst all this is going on they just forgot one teeny weeny important fact - YOU! If you are the centre of everything, why then do they not allow you to be who you want to be?

This smothering effect is continually suppressed, which eventually leads to some sort of rebellious action. This is well demonstrated in the highly acclaimed Disney Pixar animation movie Inside Out. The movie shows that all of us have different brain functions that govern our response to various situations. The functions responsible for Happiness, Sadness, Fear, Anger and Disgust are characterised and the film tells how they run the life of a young teen girl called Riley, from birth to the present day.

When a sudden change happens in Riley's life that upsets the rhythm of her emotions, the emotions try to control the situation too much, which creates more confusion for her. She rebels by running away from home to get away from all the confusion and the depression she feels. Instead of turning to her parents for help, she tries to resolve it herself. Her emotions go on an adventure in an attempt to restore normalcy is what forms the crux of this movie.

The Adolescent and Adult Brain

It is not surprising that the behaviour of adolescents would be a study in change, since the brain itself is changing in such striking ways. Scientists emphasise the fact that the teen brain is in transition doesn't mean it is somehow not up to par. It is different from both a child's and an adult's in ways that may equip youth to make the transition from dependence to independence. The capacity for learning at this age, an expanding social life, and a taste for exploration and limit testing, may all, to some extent, be reflections of age-related biology.

Understanding the changes taking place in the brain at this age presents an opportunity to get help early for a teen who may begin to suffer mental illnesses. Raising awareness in school can ensure that the child does not feel alone, that these changes and emotions are all part of growing up, especially if they feel they cannot approach their caregiver or parent to talk about it. Researching the brain may also help adults understand the importance of creating an environment in which teens can explore and experiment, while helping them avoid behaviour that is destructive to themselves and others.

SUMMARY OF WHAT YOU HAVE LEARNED FROM THIS CHAPTER

- **Fact**: The secondary years are transitional years where your hormones kick in and you change both physically and mentally.
- **Fact**: You move from being dependent to becoming independent.
- **Fact**: Due to brain changes, this is the key time that mental illnesses such as anxiety and depression are most experienced.
- **Fact**: The highest suicide rates are in this age group.
- **Fact**: We feel least supported at this time than any other time in our lives.
- **Fact:** Recent scientific studies confirm that our brain is not fully advanced until we reach our early twenties. The pain we feel emotionally has a direct effect on our wellbeing which leads to physical pain.

WHAT YOU CAN DO RIGHT NOW TO CHANGE THINGS FOR THE BETTER

- Stop blaming yourself for the past and a time you cannot change.

- Accept that period of time you lived as a teenager was a challenging time, but created opportunities that made you a stronger better person.

- Start to believe in yourself and everything you truly are. You are worth it, the value starts within you.

- Appreciate that times have changed and living in today's world as a teenager is even more difficult; however more help and support is available professionally.

- If you feel that the main issues you have emotionally were created at that time in your life, seek counselling or a psychologist to talk about your suppressed feelings. Allowing your inner child to voice any resentment and deep-rooted feelings will help heal any pain that you may be harbouring, which will in turn create your physical pain.

4

RISE UP TO RESPONSIBILITY

WELCOME TO YOUR 20s

'If you say you can or you can't you are right either way'

~ Henry Ford ~

This is a way of saying that whatever image you hold in your mind is what is going to come to pass in reality. If you think that you can do it, you will find a way to do it. If you think that you can't do it, you will find a way to sabotage yourself. It's hard to believe, but you are actually in control of what you can achieve, because it's all in your mind. The mind is so powerful that it puts limitations on itself and then you start believing those limitations. This quote by Henry Ford, helps you break free of feeling guilty, when indecision comes your way.

Our 20s are the defining decade of adulthood; 80 per cent of life's most defining moments take place from now up to age 30. By 30 more than half of this age group are married, dating or living with their future partner.

Personality can change more during our 20s than at any other decade in life. Female fertility peaks at 28. The brain caps off its last major growth spurt and the grey matter is now fully formed. When it comes to adult development, your 20s is the age when you are under construction. Even if you do nothing, not making choices is a choice all the same. It is so easy to fall into the 20 trap and make this the time you look back in your life and say they were your years of procrastination. Don't be defined by what you didn't know or didn't do back then.

American Psychologist Sheldon Kopp said: "The unlived life isn't worth examining." Too many 20-somethings have been led to believe that their 20s are for thinking about what they want to do and their 30s are for living it. But there is a big difference between having a life in your 20s and starting a life in your 20s. Even Erik Erikson, the father of the identity crisis, warned that young adults who spent too much time in "disengaged confusion" were "in danger of becoming irrelevant". This can be more said now of this generation of 20-somethings, than of any other past generation. If you want to be more intentional at work and in love, try working in an area you're curious about. Try dating someone who is different to the last person who turned out to be a disaster and try to behave a bit differently while you're at it. Sure the 20s are for experimenting, but not just with philosophies, holidays and substances.

The 20s are your best chance to experiment with jobs and relationships. This is the time that you start to put seeds down for your adult future. Then each move can be more intentional and more informed than the last. Milestones, such as your 21st, 25th and 30th birthdays, New Years and reunions are important because they trigger self-reflection. You can ask if you are where you wanted to be by this age? Ask yourself if you did what you said you would do that year. If not, ask why not. And if not now, when?

As a shrewd 20-something, I asked myself: "If you keep living your life exactly as it is, where will you be in ten years?" If you don't like the answer, now is the time to change course. It worked for me on numerous occasions and kept me on my toes.

One way to keep yourself honest about the future is by making a timeline. I remember doing this from being a child. In my primary years I read what felt like hundreds of books and I always dreamed of writing one. I believed at the age of 12 that your parents got you a Ferrari on your 18th birthday and a house for your 21st.

I did get my own house by 21, but that was because of my efforts and I'm still waiting for the Ferrari! Am I disappointed? Absolutely not, I learned and am still learning so many great lessons of life that having a super car is insignificant.

The questions I asked myself were as follows: At what age would I like to be out of this unsatisfactory job? (at that time I was working as a disillusioned 20-year-old for the Civil Service) When will I get married? How old will I be when I have my first child? How old will I be when I have my last baby?

When I was 21 and on the verge of marriage, I decided that I wanted two children by the time I was 30. I had my daughter at 28 and my son at 29. This all happened without a rigid plan - it lay hidden in my unconscious mind and when the time was right, Mother Nature kicked in automatically. When I look back and think about all my timeline predictions, I kind of got it more or less spot on, but the changes I wanted to see didn't happen overnight. Some of them took years to achieve. If you keep focused and believe in whatever you ask for, it will eventually emerge. It may sound odd to have a timeline, but you don't have to etch it in stone or tell anyone. It's just a way of thinking about how your life might, or might not, be adding up. It can save you from years of anger and disappointment which will eventually lead to the pain you feel today. A timeline helps you get clear about what you want in your life right now and in the near future. This also helps with giving yourself structure.

A timeline can be started at any age, even if you are in your 50s, 60s or 70s, you are never too old to set goals and dreams. Setting such targets gives the brain something positive to focus on, look forward to and talk about. It gives you hope in achieving and drives you towards completing what you set out to do. It sends positive messages to the body, leading to a continuum of self-healing. We need this at every stage of our life. Otherwise, what is there to live for?

Are your 20s the Selfish Years?

Some psychologists say that our 20s are the selfish years. They're when we can take time to ourselves without feeling like we're letting anyone down. You're old enough to finally buy your own alcohol and vote, but young enough to still ask your parents for money when you're too poor to afford it. It may be hard to constantly be penniless, not have any clue what you're doing with your life and eat a diet of processed food for dinner every night, but it's a time that you will never be as free as you are now or were right then. You need to embrace your selfish years before you have a job, house and children and the worry of it all.

However, if you look back at past decades when your parents and grandparents lived through their 20s, they were taking responsibility at an extremely early age. Most girls were married before their sweethearts went to war. For others, getting married young was seen as the done thing and if you were single in your late 20s, you were deemed an old maid. Queen Victoria married Prince Albert at 21; Queen Elizabeth II married Prince Phillip when she was also aged 21. I was married at 21 and still remain so after 32 years. According to the US Census 2007, which looked at the age at which women married from 1890 to the present day, the average age was 21 up until the 1990s. After then, women began to marry later - from 26.

There isn't any decade when you don't feel the pressure of responsibility. You started to understand it during your teens when you studied for your exams. The need to revise and turn up on the day to sit the test put you on the path of commitment. Our 20s allows us the freedom of choice without having to ask permission of anyone, not our parents, our siblings, our friends, or our teachers. You're now in control - or are you? It's like letting a kid loose in a candy shop! Look what happened in Charlie and the Chocolate Factory! Poor Augustus Gloop overdosed on all that sugar and was sucked away from society. If you are not careful, this could happen to you!

This is a time when your new life is emerging. You are full of hope, full of dreams of what the future holds for you, even though you're not sure in what direction it will take you. You're full of energy, passion and drive. Fear isn't an issue. In Yorkshire, where I live, they say: "Give it a go, what have you to lose?"

I'm now in my fifties and I still feel like that 20-something I once was, always willing to give things a go, always looking how to improve myself and go one better.

In your 20s it's all about how you look and gaining acceptance from society and your peers for who you are. This theme continues throughout your life – you'll want to look good in order to be accepted by your peers and society. When your needs are not met, anxiety, depression and the 'not good enough' label (the one you picked up in your childhood) makes its return.

Soon, for those who suffered bullying or domestic violence in their primary or secondary years, these words slip back into your conscious mind because you left the back door of the unconscious mind ajar. This negative state will determine whether you fail or succeed in work, relationships and, ultimately, your wellbeing.

Anxiety -The silent new disease of the 20-something living today.

If you look at the mortality rates over the last 100 years of young people living in Britain in their 20s in the first half of the century, you had a higher chance of dying before you reached 30, according to the figures provided by the Office of National Statistics. In the first half of the 20th century, it was ignorance and class division that dominated your health. The rich upper classes could afford doctors, medicine, superior jobs, good sanitation, the best food and accommodation. The poor were subjected to the opposite, hence contracting disease prematurely, which led to an early grave. Did those young adults therefore live out their life with more grit, by accepting early responsibility, making quicker decisions in order to live their dreams before they moved on?

We are now clearly living longer due to the vast improvements of medicine, money, greater knowledge, good housing and abundance of nutritious food at our finger tips. However, as in the past, the enemy of the young would be physical illness in their early years.

In the 21st century there's another silent epidemic – overthinking. Too much mental ruminating and the impact it has on the body can be seen in today's youth. Anxiety rules. As a consequence for many, this activates chemical changes in the brain that we try to correct with medication, to stop the 'free fall feeling' inside of us. For some taking a pill helps, but for the majority it doesn't. It serves only to create a dependence, a crutch, as they see it as their only way out.

However, there is a natural solution that has been around for centuries, that will restore balance in the mind and body effectively - meditation. Many people who try it, give up quickly, for fear of failing, as they struggle to connect to this simple technique. Impatient for fast results, self-sabotage comes into play just at the point when they begin to feel the benefits of what they are doing, so they stop doing it. By mastering the mind, in order to override the self-destruct button, we discover our true self. Meditation allows you to make that deep inner connection, but once again, beware. Fear may get the better of you and prevent any internal bond forming.

According to neuroscientists, as you continue to meditate your brain physically changes, redressing chemical imbalances, even though you are not aware of it re-shaping itself. Mindfulness and meditation allow the 'rest and digest' part of our nervous system to work, helping with stress management and reducing symptoms of IBS, irritable bowel syndrome. Research in people with clinical levels of anxiety found that 90% experienced significant reductions in their symptoms when they meditated.

We are all guilty of self-sabotage and using the code phrase we say repeatedly to ourselves to unlock the unconscious mind – "I'm not good enough". Everyone has their own version of it. It becomes a strong belief, a mantra locked in the mind forever.

A new breed of Pain silently developing

Obsessive Compulsive Disorder (OCD) has been around for over a century. It is categorised by the National Institute of Mental Health and the Stanford School of Medicine as an anxiety disorder. The overwhelming anxiety is what causes the characteristic symptoms that maintain OCD.

Paul Angone is one of the leading experts on the millennial generation. He coined the phrase 'Obsessive Comparison Disorder' as the new disease of the 20-somethings of our generation. Obsessive Comparison Disorder describes our compulsion to constantly compare ourselves with others, producing unwanted thoughts and feelings that drive us to depression, anxiety and discontent.

The new 20s are currently suffering a decade of high anxiety. According to Anxiety UK, one in six silently suffer. Why do you need to know this? You may be a much older and wiser person, a long way from your 20s. But you are still searching for a solution to your pain.

Obsessive Comparison Disorder is the same label as the old message of "I'm not good enough" - the limiting belief you learned from your first ten years, when your belief system was forming. If you are shaking your head and saying this isn't you, I challenge you that you did believe you're not good enough, and you still do!

Human instinct automatically carries this internal messaging system; you can't stop yourself. You do it every day in your unconscious mind without consciously knowing it. Humans constantly compare themselves to their counterparts at work, on the school run, in social activities, at the gym, in restaurants, on holiday, on the beach, with family, whilst shopping - the list is endless. We are always doing it. We walk in to an environment, new or old, with familiar or unfamiliar people around us, with our comparison mirror stored in our head. It especially shows itself during uncomfortable and challenging times, when you least expect.

So what can you do to stop the self-sabotage of "not being good enough"?

Recognise that you are not your conditioning. You have a choice. You can continue to believe the early conditioning you received and suffer over and over, or you can question what you've been taught and programmed to believe, especially if it brings you ongoing unhappiness and offers nothing for your self-realisation.

Question the expectations that have been placed upon you. Are they realistic and practical? Do they make sense to you? Do they match who you are? Are they within the scope of what you can and want to do? Because someone creates an expectation for you doesn't mean it's correct. Because you think or believe you aren't good enough doesn't mean that you aren't good enough just as you are. That's just what others may think or believe. They want you to believe that too. To counter that negative thought, create a list of the things you are and areas in which you excel, do well, or at least, are good enough.

You can ask yourself why those positive traits and accomplishments haven't been recognised and acknowledged by significant others. Are they possibly jealous of your gifts, how you look and what you have achieved? Practise not "feeding" your negative thoughts and feelings. If you refuse to add fuel to the fire, they'll eventually die down and burn out.

But if we feed them and look for evidence to support these beliefs, we make ourselves suffer. Recognise and unload the burden you've been carrying for your family (one person or all). It's their baggage, not yours. Golden Rule: Don't do for others what they won't do for themselves.

In any moment, do your best. No one else can or should question the intention you set for yourself. When you begin to define what is important to you personally, you move away from preconceived ideas about who you are, and you begin to create the person you want to be.

Helen Fielding author of Bridget Jones's Diary, demonstrates this as Bridget always battles with her image, weight and whether she is ever good enough for Mark Darcy. It is only when Mark tells her he likes her just as she is that she starts to believe in herself.

Your 20s will produce more failures than you care to remember. The key is when you fail, don't begin calling yourself a failure. Remember you are learning and growing all the time. Accept that you never stop learning about life and about yourself all your life. When you look back in later years, you can believe in what you have achieved. If you don't adopt this approach, as you enter your thirties, you will be already at a disadvantage. But you won't know it.

SUMMARY OF WHAT YOU HAVE LEARNED FROM THIS CHAPTER

- **Fact**: Your 20s is the time when you either rise up to responsibility or they can be your selfish years, as you plan how your 30s should unfold.
- **Fact**: Anxiety strikes bigger at this age, unleashing stress and depression.
- **Fact**: Meditation has a 90 per cent positive effect on improving anxiety.
- **Fact**: Obsessive Comparison Disorder becomes the new generation label for 'I'm not good enough'.

WHAT YOU CAN DO RIGHT NOW TO CHANGE THINGS FOR THE BETTER

- Start to practise mind exercises to change your limiting beliefs. These are in the form of daily gratitude, being mindful and simple meditations that create a moment of down time for the brain.
- Recognise when those self-sabotaging messages enter your mind that you need to change the old story you keep telling yourself for a new one.

- Focus on all the good things you have already achieved and start to plan ahead using your timeline.
- If you've already passed this decade, no problem, you still need to do the same action as if you are in your 20s to prevent you looking back negatively at the things you didn't do. Remember it all eventually adds up to accumulated pain, held in your muscle memory.

5

BIG DECISIONS

YOUR 30s

"Life does not owe you anything because life has already given you everything"
~ Ralph Marston ~

It's true that many people walk around as if they have something coming to them or that they're entitled to more than they already have. If they would just stop to realise that they already have everything they need for a great life, they'd have much more fun. This is a great quote to remember whenever you feel like you are missing some key element that will make your life so much better - like a new car, a fabulous holiday, a new wardrobe, Manolo Blahnik shoes... Believe me, you are not missing out, really!

You already have it inside you. You have everything you need; you just have to bring it out. With those fun, carefree days of your 20s behind you, your 30s can often feel like the real start of adulthood and the beginning of real pressure. That was the case was for me. I had been married for nine years, had two children under the age of three and had just completed a nine-month self-build project of our new home. I was 31 years old.

Never one to procrastinate, I had so much courage and inner strength at that time. Whatever challenges were at my feet, I just ploughed right through them. Maybe the reason I could do it with so much vigour and determination is because I had no fear of what the future held for me. I always believed my faith would keep me safe and if anything did go wrong, then it was meant to be. I had to deal with it, learn from it and move on. Having this approach since childhood, plus my near fatal death in my 20s from a head-on collision, allowed me not to hang on to disappointments life gave me.

For sure I got and still do get upset, as I'm quite a sensitive person and am only human at the end of the day, but with age comes wisdom, patience and experience, and we know it's not the first time and it won't be the last time for such setbacks. Life is full of them. You just have to learn how to accept them and get on with the next best thing.

I see this feeling of not being able to move on in so many of my clients. They feel stuck in their 30s and they allow negative events in their lives to bury themselves in the depths of their unconscious mind and take control. The mind is like a garden. You plant a seed that will start to grow and flourish, every time you visit the memory of that unpleasant event. If it's a negative experience, your body will produce the chemical release of adrenaline and cortisol, which, when unused, converts to lactic acid and lays dormant in your muscles. This natural body response has been produced because of your emotional connection with that memory.

Negative Thoughts

Our brain is wired in such a way that the same sensory nerves that control our movement, balance and speech, known as muscle memory, allow our emotions to travel down the same line. So every negative thought you have produces feelings of upset and pain, both mentally and physically. Remember, every time you get upset, it sends an undetectable shock wave down your body, like a minor tremor of an earthquake. It registers in your muscle memory and will affect you in the long run, either in your neck, shoulders, lower back, mid-back, head, arm, knee, bowel, stomach; the list is endless. See what happens to your body when you next have a stressful moment. You'll probably find that everything inside is tight. When you feel stressed, angry, upset or uncomfortable, you hold tension in your muscles.

Positive Thoughts

Good memories trigger happiness and healing; when you feel like this your body is in a relaxed state. It releases the chemicals of dopamine, oxytocin, serotonin – the 'feel good' hormones that support repair of damaged tissue and restoration in the body. The body is a machine; it automatically runs all your twelve major systems to maintain your existence. Its main control panel is the brain which does an amazing job.

The human brain is trained from caveman days to focus on the negative instinctively. It's your natural defence system kicking in, to protect you from getting hurt, both physically and emotionally. When someone asks you how you are, you respond that you're fine, but then continue with a negative conversation pattern. You tell them how stressed you are at work, how it's taken ages to sell your house, you can't afford a holiday, you just had a fallout with your partner, your mum's not speaking to you and, to top it all, you just broke a nail.

When we focus on the negative, on a daily basis, rather than the positive, we invite the foundations of pain to develop and form a strong base to dwell in our body. This is the start of our health problems for the future. When you give something a platform, it will begin to grow. It may take 20 years, but the damage is done, whether you are aware of it or not. For example, many people who suffered severe sunburn in the 1960s, 70s and early 80s got skin cancer in later years as a result, but at the time they didn't know about sun damage and there wasn't much sun protection around.

So dwelling on your failures, unsuccessful relationships, financial losses, job regrets, weight loss challenges and never feeling good enough, as your daily thought pattern, has the ability to impact and trigger long-term pain, illness and disease, all stored in your genetics and muscle memory.

Most people know this to be true because with any physical injury, accident or trauma, it is felt more in the later years, as the body ages, collagen breaks down, muscle strength reduces, the body shows signs of wear and tear, and pain and scar tissue become more apparent.

For example, my brother had a severe cut across his knee cap at the age of 10, whilst jumping over a stone wall. He almost cleared it, but his left knee grazed against the stone which cut his knee open. A good neighbour took him to the hospital, where he had deep stitches to seal the wound and it healed nicely, with no recurring infection or pain. Fast forward 40 years, he is now 53, and rarely a day goes by that he does not feel a deep ache from that left knee cap. The older he got, the more obvious the pain was, due to the ageing process.

So every time you visit a negative memory, which for some people can be every second of their waking day, beware! You just opened your Pandora's Box of pain, and you are adding to your body pain that will come back to haunt you in the not-so-distant future.

Looking at The Daily Negative in Your 30s

Whatever age you are, but especially in your 30s, you moan about something on a daily basis. From the minute you wake up, you complain about the weather, or the bad news on the radio or TV. You can't decide what to have for breakfast and when you do finally decide to have eggs, you don't have any in the house negative daily thoughts has produced cravings for sugary or toxic things. You know they will harm you in the long run, but for now, they meet your emotional needs and you tell yourself the diet starts tomorrow.

Alternatively, you could turn your negative thought patterns into positive ones, such as, seeing the bad weather as a joy. If it rains, it saves you watering the garden. If it's cold, it makes you appreciate your cosy home. If it's sunny, it reminds you that you're truly blessed. Turning every negative thought into a positive is a good mind game. No matter how sad or bad things are, you can find the rainbow at the end of it.

Decisions, Decisions

Regardless of what life stage you're at, if you're in your 30s, it's time to stand up and make big decisions. When you're in your 20s, it's expected that you'll make mistakes and learn from them to bridge the gap between pre-adulthood and adulthood. When you "forget" to do the laundry for a couple of weeks, or spend your whole salary on a pair of shoes, no one will give you a hard time in your 20s.

But there comes a point when you must accept and embrace the fact that you have now become an adult. You've probably made the big decision to commit to property and possibly a long-term partner and eventually children. Your finances are focused on a mortgage, your bills, dependants and, hopefully, savings.

The Disney film, Marley and Me, is a delightful comedy that focuses on the life of a twenty-something couple, who over the decades increase their responsibilities. They go from a small apartment, with small outgoings and their puppy Marley, to a large mortgage, a big house, three children, plus an ageing Marley. You witness their relationship changing as their commitments grow and their anxiety, agitation and feeling of suffocation from their obligations increase. Even though a part of them yearns for the freedom of their youth, they realise that in their most challenging years they grew as individuals the most. This is the same process for all of us. As we age, we make choices. There is no wrong or right in whatever decision we make.

One of the key areas that most people feel challenged by, at any age, is money. It's so easy to fall into the trap of financial over-commitment. We fill our homes with soft furnishings or if repairs are needed, refurbishments and essential jobs like a new bathroom and kitchen take our money. Credit cards, which may have been avoided in your 20s, become very appealing in your 30s. If you're not strict, then you fall into the credit card trap and struggle to find the 'payback' way out sign.

Unfortunately, both my husband and I naively took this 'borrow today, payback tomorrow' route. The banks were throwing their money at us in the early 1990s and in the new millennium. As we needed so much work doing on our new home, it seemed to make total sense. After all, we had equity in the property and were both earning a strong income which could fund the repayments.

But in the end only the banks and credit card companies win, just like casinos. In 2008, with high interest rates creeping in, the UK suffered one of its worst recessions since the war. We were suddenly left mopping up the mess, losing all our savings and our private health insurance and pensions, barely hanging onto our home.

This was one of the hardest periods I lived through, but I learned a lot about money and now only spend if I can afford it. When I look at today's 30 somethings, I see them living the life that I had at that age. They fund their holidays, clothes, cars and entertainment on the plastic card, turning a blind eye to the interest rates that never let them clear their debt. I urge them not to overcommit, as, at any time, it can all come crashing down so quickly.

Money & Health

Financial obligations that grow in your 30s will, over the years, have a significant effect on your mental health. We become materialistic as we buy into status symbols. If a person loves you because you wear a designer label, then they are not worth keeping.

In the film Family Man, Nicholas Cage tries on a £2,000 designer suit and suddenly feels powerful, as though he could command an audience and hold respect. He decides to buy it. His wife, played by Tea Leoni, shockingly announces that if it means so much to him, then she'll take all the savings from their children's college fund to pay for the suit. Smiling, he agrees what a good idea it is. But she is horrified and she refuses, walking away with the children.

The film demonstrates how far people will go just to attain an unnecessary product. Possessions do not make a person; it's the man who wears the suit, not the suit, that commands the power. People do feel better owning and wearing nice things, but in the end, if it creates an unhealthy situation, best lead a simple life, because, as the saying goes, the simple things in life are free.

Worrying about making and meeting repayments in your conscious and unconscious mind triggers the stress hormones adrenaline and cortisol, which can lead to lactic acid building up in your muscles. This creates ongoing aches and pains, which you blame mainly on day-to-day physical actions, such as a long time spent at the computer or working out at the gym. You never stop to consider that the negative things on your mind can create such a physical feeling of imbalance in the body, but they do.

Having a healthy approach about short and long-term commitments puts you in control of your finances and your life. Worry never resolved anything. It just creates pain, so don't go there. Everyone lives with some sort of daily pressure or pressures, but stress only produces unwanted toxins that your body does not need. They build and store inside you and eventually they create poor wellbeing in both mind and body.

When you look back at your 30s, it should be a time of growth and healthy commitment - anything less will generate pain that will be felt later in your life. It will lay dormant until enough pressure starts to push the mind and body into a different direction. This change could be sudden and unexpected, without warning, like a stroke, heart attack or collapse or it could sneak in slowly, as with depression, anxiety, skin disorders or allergies. Our 30s is the time when our bodies will change and it can be the start of a ticking time bomb for your later years, so learn to manage it well and life will be good to you.

Inner Fears, Self-Sabotage Begin to Creep Into Your Head Space

Thirty may be especially difficult because it's the first time many people realise they are ageing and mortal. For many, the first signs of grey hair, wrinkles and fine lines become more evident. In addition, some people may begin to think about achievements, goals, and failures, which can make turning thirty more daunting.

However, by confronting your impending birthday and embracing your thirties, you can not only accept, but also enjoy getting a little older. Once again your old friend – anxiety – may make you fearful about turning 30. Feeling anxiety about ageing is completely normal, but your fear might be an unrealistic reaction to getting old. Identifying why you're scared of turning 30, or any age, may help you more quickly accept a milestone. You might fear turning 30 because some people categorise it as "old." However, with medical progress and longer life expectancy, 30 is no longer middle age. You might fear turning 30 because you feel you should be taking on more responsibility and acting like an adult, or because you haven't achieved everything you thought you would by this age.

You see all your friends married, with children, getting promotions, increasing their financial wealth pot, enjoying long-term relationships, having limitless fun and endless social activities, but you seem stuck. You're still in your 30s going nowhere fast. It's okay to be on your own, with no partner, no mortgage, still dipping into the bank of mum and dad, still in rented accommodation, still in that dead-end job. If your dreams haven't come true, ask yourself why.

In the film Bridesmaids, Kristen Wiig's character has a meltdown when her best friend since childhood gets engaged. She realises everyone in her circle of friends are moving on with their lives, except her. As preparations for the big day get underway, her frustrations and negative approach to the wedding put her in a destructive state of mind. As a result, she loses her job, her apartment, her boyfriend and even her best friend.

It isn't until a distant friend comes to her rescue and reminds her that she's the reason everything in her life is falling apart. But then points out she's also the solution. The character realises that her jealousy, anger and fear of losing her best friend have manifested the wrong side of her. She decides to appreciate and value what she has right now in life and act like an adult and not a stroppy child. When she changes to a more positive attitude, everything in her life gets better and starts to flourish.

The film was a huge success. Whatever age you are, you can learn from it. We could all be the main character, as we allow our daily frustrations to dominate our day. By changing our approach to valuing the 'now', we actually live in the moment. That's what really counts.

Writing out your ageing fears will help you realise they're not rational. It could help you to accept your milestone birthday, and accept you are exactly where you should be right now. If you're older than your 30s, look back and see if you did achieve what you set out to do. Realise that many other people in your life, including your parents and probably some of your friends, have turned 30 and survived. You will easily get through your 30s and will probably enjoy the decade more than you did your 20s, if you don't get hung up on the small stuff. People say that "30 is the new 20". This behavioural tactic of framing the milestone to minimise its gravity helps you accept the ageing process more readily. If you feed anxiety through fear of the unknown, you are building your pain blocks, which will surface in your body when you least expect them, after being held in your muscle memory.

Let go of the need to be like everyone else. Just be you and if you're still not sure who that person is, then you need to go on more life journeys to find out. That doesn't mean you have to leave the country on a back-packing trip, but if that appeals to you, then do it!

The voyage of self-discovery is about getting involved in new things that are outside your comfort zone, pushing your boundaries and meeting new people. You're not changing your personality; you are just sampling what life has to offer you when you let go of the fear factor. Don't wait till you have to create a bucket list to embrace life. Experience life because you want to. No reason is required.

How Physical Changes Affect Our 30s

Whether you are male or female, your body will begin to break down in your 30s. It is Mother Nature's way of slowing you down, preparing you for a more sedentary life in the future. Your 30s is a time during which your hormones tend to balance out. This means most of the changes that happen to your body are influenced by lifestyle choices.

Skin begins to get slacker as collagen starts to deteriorate. Your muscles start to shrink in your 30s – this accelerates in later life. A desk job creates a more sedentary lifestyle which can add to an expanding waistline. Stress at work causes weight gain. High stress levels can cause a release of hormones which cause you to store weight around the middle.

Dr Marilyn Glenville discusses the effects of the stress hormone cortisol in her book, Fat around the Middle. The book draws on the latest clinical research to show that cortisol instructs the body to store fat on our stomachs to provide energy for the 'fight or flight' response to danger.

But in today's world, stress doesn't usually need this physical reaction. If you're fuming in a traffic jam or fielding work deadlines at your desk, the stored fat isn't used for fighting or fleeing – and it stays around your waist. Dr Glenville's book is an in-depth look at how your metabolism slows down and your body will take longer to bounce back, and it's well worth a read.

Take Control of Your 30s – on Your Own or With Others

When you have confidence in everything you've learned during your 20s, then you can apply this knowledge to be successful in your 30s. By cultivating and projecting confidence in yourself, you can set yourself on the path for self-acceptance and success during your 30s. Confidence comes from many sources, including knowing that you have a good education and training, good relationships, or even that you look good.

For example, if you feel that you took great care of your skin in your 20s, be confident in the fact that you probably don't have many wrinkles. You can also be confident about finishing your education or starting a good job, or even having healthy children. Yet it's important to know that even if you are confident and successful, failure is a part of the equation.

Embrace the fact that most people in their thirties feel much more confident and comfortable in themselves, which can help us enjoy ourselves and relax. Remember how you used a timeline to plan in your 20s? This can be done again for your 30s. In many cases, your goals or plans may be an extension or the culmination of what you set out to do in your 20s. Goals can help give you a concrete purpose so set some for every aspect of your life: personal, professional, and otherwise.

For example, you might want to start a family in your 30s or finally get your Master's Degree. Give yourself short and long-term goals to achieve and reassess them every year. Make plans to experience as much of life as you can through travel, education, or even just engaging with your community. Getting involved can help you forget your milestone and help you realise that your 30s are much more fulfilling than your 20s. Trying new activities can make your 30s much more exciting. Even if you don't enjoy the new things you try, you will still be more informed and versatile than you were before.

I have a lovely client in her 30s who is currently learning to play the ukulele to help her release stress and switch off her busy mind. When I asked her why she picked that instrument, made famous by George Formby, she simply asked why not. Nurturing your curiosities by allowing yourself to explore the world around you is one of the best ways to embrace your 30s. At this age, you are more likely to truly appreciate activities such as travel and trying different foods and new hobbies. You can try artistic activities such as painting, dancing, or making music; take up a new sport or engage in hobbies like photography or a book club.

Be Open Minded

Be open-minded to the new. Try activities even if they don't seem appealing at first. There is an unimaginable amount you can learn from other places, especially foreign countries and cultures. Travel will expose you to different perspectives, histories and opinions, and in turn can help you embrace your 30s. Travel will show you that the world, even if it's a nearby town, is multi-faceted and can add new sides to you, too. As you get older and wiser, you're able to recognise and appreciate the diversity around you, as well as your role in the world. Make sure to get off the beaten path when you travel. Hidden gems may surprise and enrich your experiences. Being more confident in yourself during your 30s means you'll use opportunities to travel.

I travelled a great deal in my 30s with our young family. My children's lives were enriched, as too was my own, by swimming with dolphins in Hawaii, feeling great happiness in Disney World Florida, travelling throughout Europe each summer, stopping at new destinations, and sampling each country's unique foods and what riches it had to offer. I wasn't hindered by the fear of terrorism, which is gripping today's world.

I have amazing memories of growing in my 30s, nurturing myself and creating some wonderful memories with my children. When there is so much restlessness in the world, it is time for great change, usually a change for the better.

Healthy Outlook in Your 30s

Taking care of your health is an important part of ageing gracefully and protecting your mental wellbeing. In your 30s physical recovery from injury and trauma takes longer than in your 20s. Being healthy through exercise and diet will help. Your 30s is a time for learning healthy eating habits so you meet your nutritional needs and to maintain your health and well-being. For example, you need to make sure you're getting enough protein, vitamins and fibre through foods such as lean meats or nuts, and fruits and vegetables.

Sleep is an important factor, yet we seem to lack it, due to a busy lifestyle, working late into the night and using computers and cell phones that emit electromagnetic fields (EMFs) which can create disturbances in the brain.

This was shown in a study by James Horne and his team at Loughborough University Sleep Research Centre, published on 24th May 2007.

Researchers devised an experiment to test whether cell phone signals boost a person's alpha waves, and they questioned whether these signals push people into an altered state of consciousness or have any effect on the workings of their mind. The results were surprising. Not only could the cell phone signals alter a person's behaviour during the call, the effects of the disrupted brain-wave patterns continued long after the phone was switched off, meaning the person took over an hour to fall asleep after the cell phone had been deactivated.

Although this research shows that cell phone transmissions can affect a person's brainwaves and behaviour, Horne isn't concerned that cell phones are damaging. The arousal effects which kicked in, preventing sleep, were thought to be the equivalent of half a cup of coffee. Many other factors in a person's surroundings will affect a night's sleep, as much or more, as cell phone transmissions. In a world where you are easily contacted by cell phones, never-ending emails, and social media, having unplugged alone time is vital to maintaining your mental health.

I turn off all electronics at 7pm so that I can have a few hours to myself or with my family. Try it, even for just one hour. If you can relax in that time, great - you are not suffering with electronic overload. If you find yourself restless, itching and twitching to get back on your FB page or mobile phone, then you need to review how much time you are spending with your electronic devices. One day they will make you feel ill. Too much electronic overload can stress the mind and eventually affect the body.

Making time for physical activity is as important now as it was in past decades of your life. When you were at school, you played regular sports, athletics and indoor games. Simple daily pursuits such as walking or jogging, for at least thirty minutes, can be extremely effective. Include time for rest and relaxation, such as reading a book, taking a soak in the bath, enjoying a feel good movie or comedy.

If you're short on time, HIT (High Intensity Training) is the new form of exercise proven by science to burn up as many calories as in a one-hour gym session. Using short bursts of intense movement of 60 seconds, then resting in between each burst for two minutes, is a good way of achieving a healthy body weight. If you are not short of time, then something as simple as a 3 mile run or brisk walk will give you time to work out personal or professional problems and clear your mind, while exercising your body.

Navigating through your 30s is truly a magical mystery ride, which can be enjoyed if you create goals, keep focused and be good to yourself. By giving yourself more value and respect, you open your energy to attracting better opportunities into your life and with that comes the ability to succeed and achieve.

SUMMARY OF WHAT YOU HAVE LEARNED FROM THIS CHAPTER

- **Fact**: Life is to be celebrated daily to produce feel good endorphins that heal the body.
- **Fact**: Negative thoughts produce toxic chemicals in the body, which, if unused, create pain later in your life.
- **Fact**: Positive thoughts trigger your 'feel good' endorphins which help your mind and body heal.
- **Fact**: Setting goals in your life gives your brain something to aim for.
- **Fact**: When things go wrong it's easy to blame others, but you are both the problem and the solution.

- **Fact**: Atrophy begins to break down muscle and collagen. Regular exercise and good nutrition is now vital to sustain healthy physical and mental wellbeing.
- **Fact**: Too much time spent on electronic devices will interfere with your ability to relax and affect your sleep pattern.

WHAT YOU CAN DO RIGHT NOW TO CHANGE THINGS FOR THE BETTER

- Make a list of everything for which you are grateful. When you feel negative, read your gratitude list. This will remind you to stay positive.
- If you get feelings of frustration, anger and jealousy as your friends seem to be making more progress than you, look at ways in which you can improve the areas of your life that concern you the most. Get clear, get focused!
- Reduce time spent on your mobile, computer, laptop or iPad. Having a break of 20 minutes to an hour from your devices in the day or evening will create some valuable down time for you. Remember, your electrical devices are having a relationship with you. Don't allow your mobile phone or iPad to control your life. Everything in moderation creates balance.
- Set new goals and review them annually, so you can celebrate your achievements. Put the things you haven't managed to complete at the top of your new goal list, if they're still important to you.

6

THE AWAKENING

THE REALISATION OF YOUR 40s

"The greatest discovery of any generation is that a human being can alter his life by altering his attitude"

~ William James ~

All you have to do is shift your attitude and the world around you should shift as well. If, before, you greeted each day with a sign and just trudged along and did the minimal to get by, you can change it all by greeting the day with gratitude and charging into it full steam. The world around you has to adjust to the new you, and people will look at you differently, when you are so upbeat and striving to live life to the fullest. But it all starts with an attitude change.

Your 40s is a decade of realisation and coming to terms with not only the ageing process, but reviewing where you are in your life and examining if you achieved what you set out to do. The British TV and Radio Two presenter, Chris Evans, found this such a profound time in his life that he wrote a whole book about it. In Call the Midlife he journals his struggles from this decade and how, by changing his approach with more of a positive attitude, he is able to counteract challenges. By turning a negative in to a positive and seizing his opportunities, he embraces his 50s in an optimistic way.

Again, having a timeline and setting new goals supports your fresh approach to your 40s. I always dreamed in my 20s of how and where I'd be in my 40s. Looking back, I didn't achieve all of it. I had my children and they are my greatest achievement to this day. Even though I still live in the home I built in my early 30s, I was still by my early 40s establishing the treatment that I founded. Little did I know at the time, I still had a big mountain to climb to get to where I wanted to be.

Changes in Men in Their 40s

Understanding that men and woman approach their forties in different ways can help improve our relationships with the opposite sex. As a man ages, naturally, his levels of testosterone will drop. Subsequently men can experience unwanted changes such as weight gain, especially around the abdomen, difficulty gaining and retaining lean muscle mass, depressed mood and outlook on life and a drop in sex drive. Changes in male hormone levels have been associated with a range of degenerative diseases, including heart disease, stroke, diabetes, arthritis and hypertension. Benign prostatic hyperplasia (BPH) may be due to increased oestrogen in men, and research shows that men with prostate cancer often have low levels of testosterone, which is common in their 40s.

Unfortunately, there is a triple-whammy in the hormone pool of men. Along with testosterone levels dropping, there is a rise in sex hormone binding globulin (SHBG). This means that more testosterone is bound to proteins and not available to bind with cells to exert its normal effect. Oestrogen levels also rise in men around middle age, as more testosterone is converted to oestrogen, so that they experience more of the oestrogen-like effects such as being more emotional ('softer' emotionally and physically). This can be helpful for their partners as at this stage in their life, men can sometimes bond more deeply, be more committed and less controlled by powerful sex drives of earlier years. But for many men, the changes are hard to deal with and there is a feeling of loss around them. Losing hair, losing muscle, losing libido, gaining weight and feeling weaker physically don't leave men, once the mighty provider and protector of the family, feeling on top of the world.

Changes in Women in Their 40s

Women, on the other hand, go through phases. You may be snappier at people you love, over small things that didn't used to bother you, or you may break into tears for no reason. You may feel fabulous and in love with life one day and as if you're stuck in the bleakest tunnel the next. You're not going crazy. You're going through middle age. This is a time of tremendous change, both physically and emotionally. You may be sending your children off to college, starting a new career or realising that the one you've had for years has reached a dead end.

This is the time of life when many women end long-term relationships, begin new ones or simply decide they want some time alone. It's also a time when you may be starting to deal with your parents' health issues or your own, coping with changes in your body, a sense of loss at the end of your fertility and the physical effects of the menopausal transition. For many women it's the 'wake up' call and their last chance for that first or last baby. Figures from the Office for National Statistics (ONS) show that the total number of babies born to mothers who have passed their 40th birthday has also increased year on year, from 15,066 in 2000 to 27,731 in 2010.

So it's no wonder your mood has more highs and lows than the stock market. You have a lot going on right now in your life, lots to consider. Much of it is good, but some of it may be painful or difficult (ageing parents, financial problems, relationship challenges, conception). Plus, even good things can become overwhelmingly stressful. While the occasional down day or mood swing isn't anything to worry about, if these feelings become entrenched and begin interfering with your quality of life and daily activities, you may need to have a health check with your doctor.

Positive Mental Approach in Your 40s

Life may begin at 40, but research suggests that our teens are not the only age at which we are most vulnerable to depression. Data analysis on two million people from 80 countries found a remarkably consistent pattern around the world in people in their mid-40s.

The risk of depression was lowest in younger and older people, with the middle-aged years associated with the highest risk, for both men and women, based on the study, by the University of Warwick and Dartmouth College in the US, 28th January 2008. The only country which recorded a significant gender difference was the US, where unhappiness reached a peak around the age of 40 for women, and 50 for men. Previous research has suggested that the risk of unhappiness and depression stays relatively constant throughout life. However, a peak risk in middle age was consistent around the globe, and in all types of people.

Researcher, Professor Andrew Oswald, an economist at the University of Warwick, said: "It happens to men and women, to single and married people, to rich and poor, and to those with and without children". He said the reason why middle age was a universally vulnerable time was unclear. However, he said: "One possibility is that individuals learn to adapt to their strengths and weaknesses, and in mid-life quell their infeasible aspirations".

Another possibility is that a kind of comparison process is at work in which people have seen similar aged peers die and value more their own remaining years. Perhaps people somehow learn to count their blessings.

He continued: "For the average person, the dip in mental health and happiness comes on slowly, not suddenly in a single year. Only in their 50s do most people emerge from the low period. But encouragingly, by the time you are 70, if you are still physically fit, then on average, you are as happy and mentally healthy as a 20-year-old. Perhaps realising that such feelings are completely normal in midlife might even help individuals survive this phase better."

Marjorie Wallace, chief executive of the mental health charity Sane, said: "This study raises intriguing questions about the processes that lead to depression in mid-life, as well as indicating what a common experience it is worldwide.

Depression is a complex and challenging condition that remains poorly understood, with as many as one in ten people with severe depression taking their own life.

We welcome any scientific contribution to our understanding of this illness, particularly if the research can aid the development of better treatments, both therapeutic and pharmaceutical".

Andy Bell, of the Sainsbury Centre for Mental Health, said mental health problems were extremely common, but he stressed they could occur at any time in life.

Bearing this in mind, we need to find a more positive state of mind, the older we get. We have learnt so far that emotional upset, stress, dissatisfaction and anxiety all lead to unwanted physical or mental pain.

Fast forward eight years since the research to 11th January 2016, where a new study challenges this theory. Up, Not Down: The Age Curve in Happiness from Early Adulthood to Midlife in Two Longitudinal Studies is a paper published in Developmental Psychology based on data drawn from two longitudinal studies by University of Alberta, researchers Nancy Galambos, Harvey Krahn, Matt Johnson and their team.

Contrary to previous cross-sectional studies of life span happiness, this new data suggests happiness does not pause in midlife, but instead is part of an upward route beginning in our teens and early twenties. And, according to Galambos and Krahn, award-winning Faculty of Arts researchers, this study is far more reliable than the research that came before it.

The team followed two groups, one of Canadian high school seniors from ages 18 - 43 and the other a group of university seniors from ages 23-37. Both showed happiness increased into the 30s, with a slight downturn by age 43 in the high school sample. After accounting for variations in participants' lives, such as changes in marital status and employment, both samples still demonstrated a general rise in happiness after high school and university.

Psychology professor Nancy Galambos, first author on the study, says it's crucial information, because happiness is important. It's associated with life span and overall well-being.

"We want people to be happier so that they have an easier life path" she said. "And also they cost less to the health system, and society".

Additional Factoids From the Study

- People are happier in their early 40s (midlife) than they were at age 18
- Happiness rises fastest between age 18 and well into the 30s
- Happiness is higher in years when people are married and in better physical health, and lower in years when people are unemployed
- The rise in happiness between the teens and early 40s is not consistent with a midlife crisis
- The rise in happiness to midlife refutes the claimed "U-bend" in happiness, which assumes that happiness declines between the teens and the 40s

Phillip Hodson, a psychotherapist and patron of the West London Centre for Counselling, said the findings bore out the observation that midlife could be stressful, but not as extreme as originally thought.

"Childhood and old age are protected times of life to a degree," he said. "In old age you are funded or you have funded it. It's the same for a child. You are looked after at both ends of life and your responsibilities are fewer.

The burdens of life fall on the middle-aged. You are looking after your children, your parents, yourselves. You are working as you will probably never work again in older age and probably harder than you did when you were younger. You are also having to be on call a lot, time wise, so your days are long and your purse is stretched. This is almost universally the case, regardless of whether you live in Venezuela or England".

This new discovery that people are coping better in their forties could be down to the fact that there are appreciating their time more. They are focusing on their health and mental wellbeing, meditating practising gratitude and living in the 'now' with mindfulness, which all contribute to these positive changes. Could this be the answer to an improved lifestyle, where you don't get hung up about life, and acknowledging life is good to you? Changing the way you think, with the right attitude, creates an optimistic outlook for the future and reduces pain.

The Importance of More Life-Balance

Even though we have just looked at how a positive mind set in your 40s can have an effect on your overall wellbeing, some people will stay the same. Your 40s is a time of dwindling libido due to lower hormones or exhaustion with day-to-day life. Pre-menopausal symptoms may appear, as your body changes. Your thoughts may stay the same, as you start to pick on the negative side of what forty has to offer.

You know the body is slowly breaking down. Unless you have a chef or you are a great cook and you are extremely organised, then your meals may be hit and miss. Many of us decide to eat out or eat in, choosing fast food, takeaways and ready meals, as the easy option. Traditional people will still sit down to a family meal, but if you are on your own or just a couple, then it's quicker to just grab what you can. If this is what you do most of the week, then your nutritional health will be compromised.

Your body still needs certain nutrients and now, more than any time before, your body will not let you get away with not feeding it, as you may have done in your 20s. A stream of constant pressure and stress depletes your magnesium, zinc, vitamin B and vitamin

D levels. Nutritionists recommend eating foods with omega 3 and stocking up on vitamins to combat the slump.

When we eat oily fish, nuts and seeds they provide the anti-inflammatory response we need to combat pain. Incorporating more phytoestrogens, such as fermented soya, lentils, chickpeas and flaxseed for their hormone-balancing properties.

Your alcohol consumption may now increase as a way of unwinding at the end of a busy day. You feel you can justify it as being part of rewarding yourself for a job well done or you tell yourself that you are following the Mediterranean diet.

France, Italy and Spain all have a glass or two of wine with their meal and look how healthy they are. However, they're also eating a healthy balanced meal, prepared from wholesome fresh ingredients, probably grown in their own gardens! They also have wonderful markets all year round, brimming with the most amazing selection of fruits, vegetables, fish, meats and cheeses.

I remember loving my visits to the huge hypermarkets whilst holidaying in Italy. They were filled with vibrant seasonal produce that were like colourful jewels in a treasure chest. If we had the same in the UK, our diets would be so different and obesity would be halved for sure. They get more sunshine and less rain, so they absorb better natural Vitamin D more times of the year. By the time you get to your 40s, unless you have stuck to a super diet and good solid exercise plan, then you will be at risk of some deficiency. Remember, the best way to reduce symptoms of early menopause is to exercise, cut out sugar and alcohol and keep fit in your forties.

Unexpected Physical Changes

As well as your body changing your faces changes too, particularly in women. Dr Maryam Zamani is an American trained and board certified ophthalmologist. She says the structure of our faces can change quite significantly in our 40s.

"The fat in the face can be lost and this significant volume loss can create jowls and the hallowing of the temples. The nose is affected as well, and tends to dip downwards. The lips lose volume. Facial structure can be affected with bone loss and this leaves women with sunken looking eyes and increased sagging", she says.

Botox and fillers have become so popular because woman are searching for a more youthful look and feel this is the easy solution to a long-term problem. As the body changes so does a woman's bone density. Arthritis Research UK's ageing expert Professor Janet Lord, Director MRC-ARUK Centre for Musculoskeletal Ageing Research in Birmingham, says that women should look out for their bones becoming stiff or crunching as this may be a sign of osteoarthritis, the most common form of arthritis. It is increasingly common for people to suffer it from their late 40s.

Professor Janet says: "In this condition, the surfaces within your joints become damaged so the joint doesn't move as smoothly as it should. Risk factors include genetics, obesity, age and previous joint injury".

"We don't fully understand why it's more common in older people, but it might be due to your muscles weakening and your body being less able to heal itself, or your joint slowly wearing out over time".

This decline in musculoskeletal activity can be the onset of greater physical pain.

Embracing 40 and Good Health

We know through medicine and science, that there are many changes occurring in a woman's body, so there is a great need to remain healthy. There is a renewed need particularly in the 40s to focus on being fit, as this is the time the body starts to make a noticeable physical shift. This decade is critical to making healthy lifestyle choices and changes for good – eating well and exercise will help bone mass and muscles to thrive.

Exercise helps release stress and the endorphins released during exercise will help reduce stress for a 40-year-old woman. In a woman's 20s she could sit and eat a huge tub of ice cream, munch on a mega bag of crisps or down a tray of brownies, it would go unnoticed by the body. However, no matter how appealing that still is in her 40s, it would have an effect on her weight and shape. Many women wonder why they have gained weight when they haven't changed their eating habits. It's because women have to eat differently in their 40's because of hormonal fluctuations. As they age, their metabolism slows down and the body is influenced by everything they do. Stretching and yoga, along with cardio fitness, will help boost metabolism. Healthcare providers recommend that women exercise a minimum of 30 minutes a day, five times a week. If that seems too much for you, walking or trampolining are effective too.

Today's modern women does a lot of thinking and self-reflection, writing down things to track her thoughts. Keeping a journal is great therapy. Setting out what and where they are on paper helps prioritise things, creating self-awareness which builds self-confidence leading to better decisions being made. It helps clarify who a woman strives to be, what she wants out of life and how to achieve it.

Another useful tip for women entering their 40s is getting together with similar-aged friends to compare notes and support each other, as they are all in the same boat. Relaxing with girlfriends, having fun, laughing and even crying are all good medicine.

The Best Days are Ahead

Forty can be one of the best times of a woman's life, emotionally, sexually and physically. Studies show that women aged 40 and older tend to be more confident and know what they like and need than in their earlier years. There is a decrease in dependence and self-criticism and an increase in self-confidence and decisiveness. Also, some women tend to have an increased libido at this age.

In the child-bearing days, many women feel heavier pressures and demands from children and home life. Children of women in their 40s are usually older and more independent. The days of a child clinging to Mum are behind them and women may feel more accepting, so intimacy with her spouse improves. To put it simply, a woman entering her 40s can prepare for the impending physical and emotional changes by making healthier lifestyle choices, which will make the transition years easier to accept.

Get Your 40 Winks

Sleep is essential for a person's health and wellbeing, according to the National Sleep Foundation (NSF). Yet millions of people do not get enough sleep and many suffer from lack of sleep. For example, surveys conducted by the NSF (1999-2004) reveal that at least 40 million Americans suffer from over 70 different sleep disorders and 60 per cent of adults report having sleep problems, a few nights a week or more. Most of those with these problems go undiagnosed and untreated.

In addition, more than 40 per cent of adults experience daytime sleepiness severe enough to interfere with their daily activities at least a few days each month, with 20 per cent reporting problem sleepiness a few days a week or more. Furthermore, 69 per cent of children experience one or more sleep problems a few nights or more during a week.

Sleep is a necessary human function. It allows our brains to recharge and our bodies to rest. When we do not sleep long or well enough, our bodies do not get the full benefits of sleep, such as muscle repair and memory consolidation. Sleep is so crucial that even slight sleep deprivation or poor sleep can affect memory, judgement and mood. In addition to feelings of listlessness, chronic sleep deprivation can contribute to health problems, from obesity and high blood pressure to safety risks while driving. Research has shown that most Americans would be happier, healthier and safer if they were to sleep an extra 60 to 90 minutes per night.

The American Psychology Association 'Stress in America' survey shows that stress may be interfering with Americans' sleep, keeping many adults and teens from getting the sleep they need to be healthy. Psychologist and sleep expert David F. Dinges, Ph.D., of the Division of Sleep and Chronobiology and Department of Psychiatry at the University of Pennsylvania School of Medicine, says, irritability, moodiness and disinhibition are some of the first signs a person experiences from lack of sleep. If a sleep-deprived person doesn't sleep after the initial signs, said Dinges, the person may then start to experience apathy, slowed speech and flattened emotional responses, impaired memory and an inability to be novel or multitask. As a person gets to the point of falling asleep, he or she will fall into micro sleeps (5-10 seconds) that cause lapses in attention, nod off while doing an activity like driving or reading and then, finally experience hypnagogic hallucinations, the beginning of REM sleep. (Dinges, Sleep, Sleepiness and Performance, 1991).

As statistics show that stress is one of the leading causes of sleep disruption, it is important to get into a good routine for sleep. Having earlier nights and using natural remedies such as warm baths with magnesium salts and lavender really help the mind and body relax. Stimulants such as alcohol, sugar and caffeine should be avoided after 7pm or even earlier.

In the UK, the NHS is struggling to cope with the demands for medical investigations into stress-related conditions, such as anxiety and depression. Who could have predicted by 2016 the UK would have one of the highest levels of sick leave due to mental stress? According to 2014/2015 Health & Safety Executive (HSE) statistics, 9.9 million work days were lost in the UK. Stress accounted for 35 per cent of all work related ill health cases, compared to the 1970s where stress suffered at work was only 15 percent.

Reasons behind today's work stress, anxiety, depression, poor sleep were workload pressure, tight deadlines, too much responsibility and a lack of managerial support. This pattern is not only seen in working life, but repeated in all aspects of our day-to-day living, in relationships with partners, family, friends, money, food, alcohol and health. When we look more deeply in to why, it always goes back to the connection we have with ourselves and the belief system we learned in our childhood. In order to resolve the mystery of our growing pain, our stress and our emotions, we need to look at the bigger picture.

Sleep becomes more of a problem in this decade due to the pressure we are under with commitments at home, in the family, in relationships, with finance and work. Learning to value your time more and focusing on and setting small easy step-by-step goals will help ease unnecessary pressure or stress you create inside you. Sleep not only restores the mind, but is the best anti-ageing weapon we have to fight the war against feeling old. Getting enough of this natural function is one of the key secret ingredients to being youthful and slowing down our body clock.

SUMMARY OF WHAT YOU HAVE LEARNED FROM THIS CHAPTER

- **Fact**: The right attitude is everything now
- **Fact**: Physical changes occur in the body, hormone levels for both men and women now start to decrease and change.
- **Fact**: Exercise and diet have a direct effect on wellbeing.
- **Fact**: Sleep is vital – it allows the body to repair and improve areas that are under pressure.

WHAT YOU CAN DO RIGHT NOW TO CHANGE THINGS FOR THE BETTER

- Positive attitudes help overcome feelings of depression. Focusing on the good things you have in your life heals you mentally.
- Ensuring your diet becomes more structured and you regularly exercise will help stop bad habits creeping in. Fluctuating weight will be harder to shift in the long run. Start becoming more aware of how your body is changing and help maintain a healthy approach.

- Get regular 7 to 8 hours' sleep. Unwind with a book or warm magnesium bath to relax tense muscles. Lavender helps ease the mind and is a natural way to fall asleep.

- Your forties are all about a good positive attitude, celebrating your achievements and setting new goals for the next decade.

- Take any additional vitamin supplements to support mind and body.

7

THE ALL OR NOTHING YEARS

YOUR 50s & 60s

'Your time is limited so don't waste it living someone else's life'

~ Steve Jobs ~

Even if things are looking grim, you can still keep your eyes fixed on your dreams. In fact, when things aren't going well, it is the perfect time to keep your focus on something that makes you feel good. The thing most people do is feel bad when things are bad and feel good, when things are good. But the trick is to feel as good as you can, even when things aren't going the way you want them to, because that speeds up the process of getting them back to the way you want them.

The book The Secret teaches us this valid point: that what you focus on, you create. I decided to apply this positive attitude and take a dose of my own medicine, when reaching the end of my current book deadline. My proof reader was going on holiday, as was my editing team, so if I missed my deadline with them, everything would fall apart and my September book launch would have to be extended into October, missing all the press.

I suffered continual interruptions in my timetable, and the setbacks with my writing started to build a frustration bubble inside me. I had six days to complete three chapters and it was beginning to generate physical symptoms, such as a tight chest, tense shoulders, aching neck, sciatic pain on my right side, and hot and cold flushes. You may think that these symptoms were caused by long hours, day after day sitting at the computer, feeling vexed.

We always look for the physical reasons for our physical pain. When you're happy doing something, your body and mind are in a relaxed state. When you're in a stressed state, your physical body becomes tense. Let's set the scene. I was happily penning my third book. I love writing and researching and I was comfortable in what I was doing work-wise. My conscious mind was therefore fully engaged in the task. It was the other part of my mind that was pre-occupied with my commitments to my family, which was beginning to influence my physical state.

All these signs were as a result of my emotional thinking pattern, transmitted from my unconscious mind. I was sort of aware it was happening, but chose not to break my concentration and give it any more thought. Your obligations in life are stored in the unconscious mind. Mine was preying on my busy conscious mind, which was trying to focus on the task at hand. My body kept telling me to calm down, breathe and pace myself, but my mind felt like it was a racehorse in the Grand National. I was hoping to cross the finish line without any injuries on the way. Looking at my pain using the principles of LT Therapy, my right shoulder pain was being caused by my commitment to caring for my mother with dementia. My lower right sciatica was my inner child, fearing I wouldn't reach my deadline date, and my left shoulder and neck were my family, whom I was neglecting, which upset me intensely. I was producing bucket loads of adrenaline, due to my negative thinking in a sedentary position, hence the muscular aches and pains.

Targets and deadlines seem to be constant in my 50s (I'll be 53 when this book is launched September 2016). I know when I was in my 20s I set goals and continued to do so in every decade, but they were positive tools to enable me to move forward. It seems as you get older, the To Do lists, checklists, deadlines and targets go on forever and ever. They can become overwhelming if you don't get the balance right and I need them more than ever now, as my memory often fails me, a symptom of the menopause no doubt. Sometimes I feel like the Andrex puppy chasing the runaway toilet paper, never catching the end of the roll!

Time - Use It Wisely or Lose It Forever

So much of these frustrations are to do with a commodity we never seem to have enough of - time. Time is wonderful if you master it. When you are young, time goes so slowly, but when you are getting older, it goes too fast. Why? Because you haven't mastered it. But I haven't got time to master it you shout! Yes, you do, you only need to look at your 24-hour clock to see why you feel there is never enough time.

Time is our test, time is our healer, time is our luxury. It's our joy, happiness and peace. Time is a service that runs 24 hours a day, 365 days a year continually. Use it wisely or lose it forever. You can't take time back. Once it's gone, it's gone, so appreciate every second Father Time gives you.

When you are calm and still, you have made the time to watch the world go by. This happens when you have mastered meditation, mindfulness and gratitude, which can take a moment, not necessarily a lifetime. You stop time, by appreciating and valuing your surroundings, your daily actions, people, the weather, nature and food.

Most of you don't give yourselves this treat of time out. You're too busy, rushing around, trying to do all the housework before you go to work, fitting the shopping in after work, dashing to the doctors, dentists, schools, seeing the grandchildren, before catching your breath at bedtime. When you are in your 20s, your mind races like a Ferrari. By the time you hit your 50s and 60s, your mind is still racing like a sports car, but your frame, that's your body can't keep up. The mind and body have to synchronise, or the division creates a rift in your wellbeing. It's like driving a car in the wrong gear. Eventually you are going to wear down the bearings. In your body the bearings are your bones and muscles, and wearing them down leads to aches and pains.

Learning to appreciate and accept time as your ally, not your enemy, means your pace of life starts to slow down for the greater good. Suddenly, you've come off the merry-go-round and can begin to enjoy the gentle views the Big Wheel has to offer. You can now value what's around you and see clearer ahead of you. You have prevented the feelings of being overwhelmed, deflected anxiety and improved your overall wellbeing.

If you allow yourself the freedom of slowing down, you give yourself the gift of time, not because of your age, or because society says you have to, or because you have a life threatening disease, but because you understand you need to be calmer. You might argue you give yourself lots of time, but when you really look at it and break it down, do you give yourself quality time?

History has so many good examples about using time effectively. I have always loved world history, especially the lessons that the wars produced. A need to appreciate how nations came together to conquer criminal human behaviour and the resilience of innocent people, who fought against such atrocities, made them value their time. War was a period of famine and starvation; human life lived on borrowed time.

My parents always talked about their early childhood, which was during the Second World War and how hungry they were, to the point of starvation; there was never enough food. People prioritised their time and those who survived became great humanitarians. The actress Audrey Hepburn is remembered as being one of Hollywood's greatest film icons, as well a huge ambassador for the United Nations International Children's Emergency Fund (UNICEF). This charity organisation was founded in 1947, and has been working to improve children's lives ever since. It has many programmes that reach out to the different needs of children all over the world. She worked diligently to raise awareness of the poverty children suffered.

In her own childhood she experienced the painful effects of war. Her parents moved the family from Belgium to the Netherlands, believing it would not be invaded by the Germans, but unfortunately by 1940 they had occupied The Netherlands. Life became increasingly difficult and by 1944 the war had created a food shortage. The Dutch famine, known as the Hongerwinter (Hunger winter) in Dutch, was a famine that took place in the German-occupied part of the Netherlands, during the winter of 1944–45, near the end of the war.

A German blockade cut off food and fuel shipments from farm areas. Some 4.5 million were affected and survived because of soup kitchens. As many as 22,000 died because of the famine. Many people had to fight premature diseases. Audrey Hepburn developed acute anaemia, respiratory problems and oedema, as a result of malnutrition. Grateful for her own good fortune, after enduring the German occupation as a child, she dedicated the remainder of her life to helping impoverished children in the poorest nations.

When you have too much of something, you take it for granted and when you have so little, you want more. Time becomes extremely important in these decades when we want to make the most of it. The danger is to fill every second with the things we believe we need. We totally miss the point of valuing the moment.

The British romantic comedy film - About Time, written and directed by Richard Curtis, shows the importance of time. The story is based on a 21-year-old boy called Tim, who realises that he has the ability to travel through time. He uses this ability to change several situations of his life. Although all of time is at his disposal, he begins to cherish each day, as if he travelled to that day specifically to enjoy it again. He learns at the end of the film that he can't change certain events, like his sister's accident or his dad's death, as he cannot change their destiny, only his own. So he focuses on appreciating each day as if it were his last. When you plan your day, even when you are under immense stress or you are battling with your health or the health of a loved one, never forget to take a moment of time to acknowledge your presence in the day and how you contribute in some way to making the world a better place.

Time travel has always intrigued people. I remember the original 1960 film, The Time Machine, with Rod Taylor playing H.G Wells, a scientist and inventor who makes a time machine to travel back to the past, as well as forward to the future. The film was ahead of its era and inspired stories linked to time travel. Some of my favourites are Back to the Future, A Moment in Time, Groundhog Day, Déjà vu, When Peggy Sue got Married and The Time Traveller's Wife.

One of British television's biggest success stories is Dr Who, which regularly attracts millions of viewers. The doctor has many adventures travelling through a multi-dimensional time frame, battling war lords and aliens and my particular favourites, the Daleks. Time travel continues to fascinate people, even the well-respected physicist and cosmetologist, Stephen Hawking, wrote about how to build a time machine in the Daily Mail newspaper on 27th April 2010. Mr Hawking stated anything is possible. After all, not so long ago people didn't believe a man could go to the moon, but he eventually did.

The importance of Investing in You

The older you get, the faster the sand grains in the hour class run, so how can you slow down time in order to benefit from what you have achieved? You're at an age to recognise that products and holidays are great whilst they last, and they make you feel good for that moment, as do gorgeous gourmet food and delicious cocktails. You take nothing for granted, but you know they are not the solution to problems, nor do they remove difficult obstacles in your daily life.

You learned in your earlier years that being seduced by such riches never solved anything. The difficulties are still there when you get back, the only difference being that you are probably in a better frame of mind to deal with them. Even the wealthiest people don't enjoy such luxurious pleasures anymore. The majority of people who reach their 50s and 60s are now looking for a bigger purpose in life. They are searching for the answer to the bigger questions of what, why and when.

It's never too late to invest in yourself, particularly this decade. I have always been inspired by people who excelled in later life. Colonel Saunders didn't perfect his famous chicken recipe till 65. Laura Ingalls Wilder didn't write her series of well-loved books Little House on the Prairie until she was in her 60s. Charles Darwin didn't publish his theory of evolution until he was 50. Ray Kroc didn't start the McDonald's corporation until he was 52. John Pemberton didn't invent Coca Cola until he was 55, so there's lots to play for. For me, my 50s were the right time to go back to my first love - education.

In September 2016, I will be starting my Master's Degree in Science, specialising in Advance Complimentary Medicine. It's a three-year research degree and I should graduate on my 56th birthday. I will still be running my dual clinics, which will assist my study, as well as investing in researching new medicine. The knowledge I will gain will help support not only my present clients, but people around the world, helping them understand how to be healthier, and how to self-heal and become pain-free. Use these decades to inspire yourself. Now is the time, as Jennifer Lopez sings in Get Loud, to drop the "It's too late" act and stop worrying about how life is running past you. Life is running with you, side by side. It's your new best buddy, so spend it wisely.

Control Your Pain or Pain Will Control You

You've conquered financial drawbacks, become more established in society, grown in your career and by now, you've probably got all the trinkets you wanted in your 20s 30s and 40s. You're at the point of starting to relax a little, just when those physical signs of ageing creep in again. All those aches and pains that occurred infrequently in your 40s now become a daily presence in your 50s onwards.

There are two ways of approaching pain. There are those people who choose to just get on with life, shift their focus on moving forward, and don't allow their pain to preoccupy their mind or become part of their negative thinking pattern. Then there are people who constantly complain about it and give it permission to be there. What they are doing is allowing their pain to take control of a part of their brain that always looks for pain in the body. Pain is like a squatter. It has no right constantly being there, but as long as you allow it, by focusing on it and with negative thinking, it will make the most of its stay. Recognising that you have a choice when it comes to pain means you are in control of pain, rather than pain being in control of you.

There are also people who have been so caught up living everyone else's life that they have forgotten about themselves. Commendable, but being the sacrificial lamb did nobody any favours. Eventually you become resentful and ungrateful. If that's you, when it comes to treating yourself, you will feel guilty, as you are not used to it. My sister did just this. She is such a wonderful person who helps with the care of our mother; she's a great aunty to my children, a conscientious worker in her job, a supportive wife and good listener to her friends. She was so busy being busy, she forgot about taking time out for herself. She was forced to take annual leave from work or she would lose it.

Her husband seized the opportunity to book a last-minute break overseas. For some people jetting off to a hotter country would be an exciting prospect. For others, like my sister, who prefer to plan ahead, this was a nightmare. She likes to have time to book the cat into the cattery, look for a new summer wardrobe and search for a good price break. When it comes to planning she gets A plus; she's the best planner I know, at times even beating me! But she plans for everyone, except herself. We self-sabotage our time by focusing on everyone and everything, except ourselves.

If this approach is not changed, then your 50s and 60s are a time when you can become more cynical about life. You can become grumpy about everyone and anything, feeling that life let you down, rather you letting yourself down. The BBC hit comedy series - One Foot in the Grave, about a fictional character called Victor Meldrew, epitomised the archetypal grumpy old man aged 60.

He looks at life so negatively, that everything he does goes wrong to such an extent he coins the phrase: "I don't believe it". He is a man simply misunderstood because of the way he presents himself. He is always perceived as grumpy and we start to think of our 60s as time when we're all like this.

Remembering what's important about this time - your health. Without it, you'll struggle to enjoy life, look after your loved ones or, in some cases, function at all.

Feeling Fit, Looking Fabulous

Ageing speeds the very decline we dread most. And it ultimately robs our life of any meaning, due to the aches and pains that start to dominate our body. No wonder there's an attitude shift in the making. We now live and die, psychologically and spiritually incomplete. It may be a troubling sense of incompleteness that stirs an appreciation for age even though we're the generation that invented "having it all". We fear and deny ageing, because we fear and deny death. In our denial of death and the ageing of the body, we have rejected the wisdom of the aged, and in doing so, have robbed old age of its meaning and youth of its direction.

We pretend that old age can be turned into an endless middle age, thereby giving young people a false road map to the future, one that does not show them how to plan for their whole life, gain insight into themselves, or to develop spiritually. Men in these decades are now commonly seen with a younger partner, as they secretly fear ageing the most. Their youthful partner reminds them that they still have what it takes to be a young man again.

The signs of denial and anxiety over ageing permeate every aspect of our lives. We have great models for naturally growing old gracefully, such as Helen Mirren, Joanna Lumley and Jane Seymour. Flip the coin and you have growing old cosmetically in the case of Jane Fonda, Sharon Osbourne and Joan Rivers.

People turn to cosmetic surgery to do battle with ageing. In the USA in just two decades, from the 1960s to the 1980s, the number of rhytidectomies, wrinkle-removing face-lifts, rose from 60,000 to an estimated two million a year at an annual cost of $10 billion.

According to The American Society of Aesthetic Plastic Surgery, Americans spent more than 12 billion dollars on surgical and non-surgical procedures in 2013. The negative view of ageing is reinforced by the media. Articles and advertising never show a mature model, even in displaying fashions designed for women over 50. One of the only few successful models of our time who campaigns for the older woman is Twiggy, now in her mid-60s, a great example of how amazing women can be at any age.

It's this thirst for youthfulness, focusing too much on the external superficial side of our body that allows us to become lost in what is happening on the inside of our body. We may be less observant, or turn a blind eye and ignore early warning signs of illness. I don't particularly look forward to my smear test or breast checks, but I see them as a necessary part of ageing. It is my responsibility to attend these appointments, as well as my annual women's health check at my doctor's surgery.

According to NHS Choice published 15th January 2014, women between the ages of 50 to 65, who did not attend screening tests as recommended, were six times more likely to develop cervical cancer at these ages compared with women who did. Ageing internally causes the external symptoms of slackening skin and decrease in collagen. As you get older, your tendons become less elastic and are more prone to injury. Ease your aches. Use 'RICE', which stands for rest, ice, compression, and elevation. Take a break from activities that aggravate your joints. Put an ice pack on the sore area. Wrap it in a bandage, and prop up the area (for example, put your leg on a pillow or two if your knee hurts). Take an NSAID, a nonsteroidal anti-inflammatory medicine, like ibuprofen or naproxen, to ease inflammation. Talk to your doctor if you're not improving after a week as recommended by NHS Choice.

Let's Embrace the Menopause

Women entering menopause today are healthier, feel younger than their years, and lead more active lives and careers than previous generations. However, this can be an uncomfortable and confusing time. Women are plagued with hot flashes, irritability, headaches, depression, sleepless nights, and fatigue, as well as a waning libido and decreased ability to enjoy sex. During your 50s, the journey into the menopause begins. Some women notice signs as early as their mid-40s, but every woman has different experiences.

Most of the changes in your body during this decade are related to the menopause. Why do we dread it so much? Probably because we fear what it brings – it's a bit like Christmas chocolates. There will always be some parts (the coffee and strawberry creams, the Turkish Delights and hard toffees) that no one wants.

From a medical point of view, The Royal College of Obstetricians and Gynaecologists says, overall, evidence shows that the alternatives to HRT such as complimentary therapies and herbal remedies are much less effective at easing the menopause symptoms as HRT. The best ones can reduce the severity of symptoms by 50% to 60%, compared with a reduction of 80% to 90% with HRT. So what can you do to help you support your symptoms and reduce pain?

1. There's no Reason to Struggle

Women will most likely spend a third of their life peri-menopausal or post-menopausal. Considering how much you've been through in your life, there is no reason to suffer the discomforts of menopause. Most people see it as normal. They take various medicines for arthritis pain, cardiac and vascular disease, and diabetes, so why not also evaluate and/or treat the symptoms and changes that come with menopause? There are plenty of options available now, besides hormone replacement therapy (HRT). Doctors are now embracing integrated medicine to accomplish what works best for each individual woman, whether it includes HRT or not. One of the newer products they are recommending is Oöna, a herbal supplement that combines black cohosh and chaste tree berry.

2. There is no "Right" Way, Just "Your" Way

You may believe that HRT is either the "fountain of youth" or the "fountain of evil." Truthfully, it's neither. Be informed about all the options available and consult your doctor. With an open mind and effective communication, you and your doctor will find what works best for you. There are several approaches, including conventional medications, herbs, acupuncture, and meditation.

My mother took HRT for over 25 years and it was her 'elixir of youth'. Unfortunately, she made the decision to come off it five years ago at the age of 76, due to another HRT scare in the UK that saw millions of woman panic. My poor mother aged almost overnight by 15 years. Her joints and muscles instantly filled with pain. She suffered an average of 20 hot flushes a day. She became frail and fragile within two years and her hair thinned.

A study published in the Pulse, the leading journal for GPs in the UK, advised GPs to ignore the latest scare. The analysis of the Women's Health Initiative showed a possible risk reduction in women taking oestrogen-only HRT, who were aged 50-79 and had a hysterectomy. The Royal College of General Practitioners, (RCGP) spokeswoman on Woman's Health, Dr Sarah Jarvis, was concerned another outbreak of hysteria would further tarnish a therapy that had the potential to vastly improve a woman's quality of life.

When considering any medication, if it improves your quality of life, then that is what ultimately matters. For example, painkillers temporarily support the body, by blocking the pain receptors. Eventually the body gets used to them and over the long term, they stop working.

The female hormone oestrogen naturally occurs in a woman's body. HRT mimics and replaces that loss at menopause, but as it's replacing a natural hormone that was always part of the body, it continues to work.

For many women HRT has been a lifesaver, restoring them back to their former selves. If I knew then, what I know now, then maybe I would have encouraged my mother to stay on the HRT. Her dementia came on two years later after coming off HRT which makes me wonder if the extra oestrogen gave her some protection.

A study carried out by the University of California, funded by the National Institute of Ageing and Health 2013, reported that taking HRT could delay the onset of Alzheimer's and dementia, as oestrogen helps protect the neurons in the brain, restoring female hormone levels.

3. Update Your Vitamin Regime

If you have been taking the same multivitamin for years, now is the time to review the label. Women in midlife have different needs and should take at least 400 IUs of vitamin E (take these in 200 IU intervals), 400 mcg of folic acid, 100 mg of vitamin B6, 1250-1500 mg of calcium with 500 mg of magnesium, 200-1200 IUs of vitamin D, and 1,000-5000 mg of vitamin C with Rose Hips. Omega 3 essential fatty acids are also very important and can be found in good oily fish, Chia seeds and flaxseed. The charity, Age UK, recommend a healthy balanced diet, but a busy life can often mean you miss out on essential vitamins, so supplement wherever needed.

4. Hormones are Affected by Stress and What we Eat

As production of oestrogen, progesterone and testosterone by the ovaries declines, the adrenal glands, muscles and brain begin to produce an increasing percentage of the body's androgen hormones and convert them to weaker oestrogens. A healthy diet and positive attitude have been shown to help this conversion. Also, symptoms of menopause are known to have "triggers" such as alcohol, caffeine, sugar and spicy foods, which you should eliminate or cut back on. Starches should come from darker whole breads, grains and vegetables. It's also a good idea to eliminate, or deal with, as much stress as possible since most women feel either a greater number of menopausal symptoms or feel them with greater intensity when they are under stress.

5. There is Usually More Than a Hormonal Shift

Often there is an accompanying emotional shift. As Christiane Northrup, M.D. points out women focus much of their energy during the child-bearing years on caring for others. As they move towards menopause, the focus commonly turns to caring for themselves. Women often re-evaluate their lives and their relationships, looking for the understanding, support and the encouragement they feel they've been giving others for so many years. Make sure that you are not asking someone to read your mind and take care in how you express yourself. If you need help, consult a doctor or therapist. Keeping negative emotions stored will only result in physical pain.

6. Diet - Making the Best of the Four-letter Word

You may feel that your eating habits haven't changed or that you're even eating less, but find yourself gaining weight. In mid-life women experience a 10-15% metabolic rate slowdown. Their bodies become more efficient at storing energy as fat, and as oestrogen levels fall, appetite increases. After menopause, this weight usually goes away as metabolism re-stabilises, but in the meantime, keeping blood sugar level during the day by eating small meals tends to help most menopausal women. The key is not to overeat at night as metabolism peaks earlier in the day. Cut down on carbohydrates and have protein with each meal. A new study published on 28th August 2015 by researchers at the University of Birmingham showed that drinking a glass of water 30 minutes before a meal helped with weight loss.

7. Exercise Makes Every List

Regular aerobic exercise can help ease menopausal symptoms, support heart heath and maintain metabolic rate. A programme of weight or resistance training will help maintain bone strength. There are so many different ways to exercise, from tai-chi to spin. The key is to find one or two that you enjoy. I wrote a whole chapter in my first book on the benefits of rebounding. It's a fun exercise that ticks all the boxes in achieving weight loss, muscle tone and great all-round fitness.

8. Hormones and the Libido

A deficiency in oestrogen or progesterone can cause changes such as vaginal dryness and thinning of the vaginal wall, making sex less pleasurable and even painful. Testosterone levels also fall during the menopausal transition and can add to a decreased sex drive, lower energy and a lower sense of well-being.

Most physicians will prescribe an estriol cream for the vaginal dryness and thinning of the wall. Similarly, if low testosterone levels are detected, supplementation to normal levels is easy to achieve. Additionally, the combination of the herbs black cohosh and chaste tree berry found in Oöna will also help with vaginal dryness and thinning vaginal walls.

9. You Can Keep Your Skin Radiant

First, if you smoke, here's another reason to quit. Smoking damages your skin and most smokers see wrinkles earlier in life. Smokers will also enter menopause earlier. Make sure you use a face cleanser that is cream-based, since soap or gel cleansers tend to dry out middle-age skin. Exfoliate once a week and mask once a week (not on the same day). Finally, supplement with omega 3 fats like flaxseed oil and/or primrose oil. Vitamins C and E are also very important, as is coenzyme Q10. Water and fibre are also very important for your skin and body.

10. Keeping Your Mind Sharp and Heart Strong

The more the link between oestrogen and cardiovascular disease is investigated, the more apparent it becomes that the cardiovascular protection oestrogen has been thought to offer, may not apply to everyone. In fact, it shouldn't be given to women with a history of cardiovascular disease.

As for the mind, it is difficult to determine if a woman's feelings of scattiness and forgetfulness are caused by diminishing hormones, as opposed to stress or ageing. It appears that a minimum amount of oestrogen is essential for certain memory functions. Also, good health habits have led to improved memory function. Eat at least five servings of fruits and vegetables per day, supplement with B-vitamins, E and zinc, and get plenty of antioxidants such as vitamin C. Ginkgo Biloba can also help, but it's important to choose a reliable brand and look for standardised extracts.

Whether you are symptomatic or not, menopause is a great reminder to take a serious look at your health. As modern medicine has now extended our life span to almost twice what it used to be, our bodies undergo profound physiologic changes. The importance of the mind-body connection cannot be underestimated and choosing to deal with what ails you is a big first step.

Find an approach to menopausal symptoms that you are comfortable with and works for you, and you can begin to spend this time focusing on the positive aspects of this transitional time, instead of suffering unnecessarily. This is an opportunity to make adjustments that could ensure that the years to come are most enjoyable. You've earned it.

Keep Lean & Clean

Weight matters, it contributes to physical pain. As I became bogged down with unexpected responsibilities as a carer for my mum with Dementia, I was still running my two 50 hour a week clinic's, both in London and Bradford. I was blessed that my children were enjoying independent living, my years of teaching them how to cook, clean and be adaptable to their surrounding had paid off.

By becoming well known for what I had founded, LT Therapy, my brand became popular globally. There was even more demand to meet my responsibility to my clients and readers around the world. I knew that there was only one of me and even though I was brilliant at organising my days, meeting my targets and doing all my admin, something had to give. For me, it was the silent sabotage of my body weight, I watched and waited. I was using food as my emotional comfort blanket and knew what I was doing.

I had been here many times in my past, enjoying the security of what processed sugary foods gave me, yet really punishing myself for my success.

I knew about what all the bad stuff was doing to me, but I still did it. I was like a person in a bad relationship, who keeps breaking up with the abusive partner, then goes back for more. When you reach a point of success, whichever decade you achieve it, for most people, they have a fear of success, which goes back to their conditioning in their childhood days, of not being good enough.

I was beginning to fear my own success which is crazy. You work all your life to help people and you love what you do, but with that dedication comes success and I feared it. I know why. All my childhood years and young adulthood, I was being constantly told by my father that I was not good enough, would never amount to anything and would contribute to nothing (he never put it that nice, that's the clean version). If you were ever told that by your parents, teacher, peers, you can be certain that you will feel uncomfortable with success, until you accept that you are good enough. It's a proven reason why we self-sabotage success and fail. I managed to publish the book and correct my limiting belief, losing the stone I had put on.

Shona Wilkinson, a nutritionist from SuperfoodUK.com believes that pain is often an expression of inflammation in the body and that you should be able to manage your pain naturally. She and fellow experts show how you can reduce pain and inflammation in the body, simply be changing your diet;

Eat your Five a day - You all know about the importance of this fact, it is well documented. One of the most important aspects of reducing pain and inflammation in the body, is to ensure good acid-alkalisation in the blood. (I learnt this in 2001 with Tony Robbins) It's also beneficial to your general health and wellbeing.

Fats - Fats in your diet are metabolised in the body and turned into 'local hormones', known as prostaglandins. Depending on the type of fat, these local hormones can either increase inflammation or reduce it. There is evidence to show Omega- 3 fats reduce and Omega -6 fats can increase inflammation. Dr Marilyn Glenville, a leading nutritionist and author of 'Natural Alternatives to Sugar', said: 'Good sources of omega-3 fats are oily fish such as salmon, trout, sardines, mackerel and halibut.

Protein - Protein is essential for repair and healing in the body, but high levels of protein from meats may actually have the opposite effect. Eating more vegetable proteins such as beans, lentils, chickpeas, fermented soya (tempeh or miso) and nuts and seeds. Fish is a good protein, organic eggs, chicken and turkey in moderation.

Spice - Include plenty of gentle spices in your meals. The spices turmeric, cayenne and ginger are known to have an anti-inflammatory action in the body. If you don't like added spice in your food, then taking a supplement that contains it you will benefit from CurQuMax by Quest Vitamins.

Water - Water transports nutrients to where they are needed in the body and removes toxins, waste products and dead cells, which are produced in higher quantities when there is inflammation. Most people are dehydrated daily, hence they feel more aches and pains caused by inflammation they are carrying in the body. Drinking enough water as recommended, eight glasses, per day, will help reduce these symptoms of pain.

Food & Drink to be Avoided - Diet has a major impact on inflammation in our body. Say no to the following and feel the benefits;

- **Sugary foods and refined carbohydrates** - Sugar is especially acid-forming and pro-inflammatory. Refined carbohydrates – white bread, pastries, pasta, pizza etc. – break down quickly into sugars when digested so are just as problematic. Don't forget about alcohol - it is the most refined carbohydrate!
- **Coffee**
- **Fizzy drinks** - they are either high in sugar or artificial sweeteners

- **Red meat, organ meats** (e.g. liver, kidney, heart, brain) and game meats (venison, pigeon, goose). They are acid forming and high in the pro-inflammatory arachidonic acid
- **Saturated fats** – found mainly in red meats, full-fat dairy products, fried foods, sausages, meat pies, etc.; and hydrogenated and 'trans' fats found in margarine, poor-quality refined cooking oils and many other processed foods
- **Citrus fruits**, especially oranges and orange juice, can worsen symptoms in some inflammatory conditions such as arthritis
- **Nightshade family vegetables** may exacerbate pain and inflammation for some people, especially those with arthritis. These include tomatoes, white potatoes, aubergine and peppers

Stress - Stress causes acidity in the body and increases free radicals, contributing to pain and inflammation. Sugary processed food, spikes your blood sugar and increases acidity in the body. When you get stressed, you crave these foods or drinks containing sugars, so inflammation and pain follows. Poor sleep will also affect your blood sugar increasing acidity in the body. Remember a more acidic body, the more you will feel your aches and pain. If you don't get enough sleep, you can find it harder to adapt to challenging situations and concentrate. When you can't cope as efficiently with stress, it can be harder to have a good night's rest. Magnesium is known as 'nature's tranquiliser' and is needed to relax our muscles and nerves, which helps us to fall into a peaceful sleep. To ensure you're getting enough magnesium, try and include plenty of magnesium-rich foods in your diet such as, pumpkin and sunflower seeds, fish and leafy green vegetables. There are also many good supplements available on the high street you can add such as, KalmAssure Magnesium Powder by Natures Plus.

Avoid Weight Gain

Additional weight puts pressure on the skeletal, your bones. The impact of this unexpected change that either crept in over the years or suddenly materialised within a short space of time, only adds to your overall pain. I noticed with the pressure of the extra weight my body had to carry around, I was beginning to ache more. My legs became heavier, feet puffier, I was struggling to keep as active as normal.

Being overweight, can make just getting around a challenge. Compared with people at a healthy weight, those carrying extra pounds have a harder time walking a quarter-mile, lifting 10 pounds and rising from an armless chair, even tying their shoe laces, that's why slip-on's are such a comfy option. The burden of these problems appears to be greater than in years past, probably because people are now obese for a greater portion of their lives, according to experts.

Excess weight plays a role in so many common and deadly diseases. Being overweight and obese can cut years off your life. A New England Journal of Medicine study, that followed more than half a million 50- to 71-year-olds for a decade found an increase of 20% to 40% in death rates among people who were overweight at midlife. Among obese people, the death rate was two to three times as high.

A 2010 study in the same journal, which pooled findings from 19 studies that followed nearly 1.5 million white adults, 19 to 84 years old, for a similar period of time, found that the risk of death, increased along with body size, ranging from 44% higher for those who were mildly obese to 250% higher for those with a BMI of 40 to 50, classed as morbidly obese. Learning to watch your weight at this time of your life, will pay dividends in the long run and help reduce symptoms of the menopause and pain.

As you begin to age, your muscle fibres become less dense, which makes them less flexible and more prone to injury and soreness. You may be prone to soreness after activities you used to do with no problem, like gardening or exercise. You're more likely to get a muscle strain with every passing decade. The best thing you can do is to try to avoid hurting yourself in the first place, by not lifting, pushing, or pulling heavy items without help. Stretching and exercises like yoga and Pilates can help keep your muscles long and limber, and can help when you're feeling sore, too.

Dealing with Grief

Grief, bereavement and loss are among the biggest, most uncontrollable feelings we experience at any age and they will impact all aspects of your life.

The year 2016 will be well remembered, not only for being the year we lost the most celebrities in death, but for the losses we had among family and friends. I feel very sad and heartbroken that that person who has been a part of my life is no longer in it. Whatever that person was to me, I will always remember them, not with tears - that only creates deep emotional and physical pain for me, but with respect and love, by celebrating how they made my life better, richer and happier. I know then, as they look down on me, that the life they lived meant something.

I recently had the pleasure of working with a family of three - a father and his two daughters. When they came to me, he was not sure why his two lovely daughters had brought him to my clinic for his Father's Day gift. He didn't know who I was and what my background entailed. I explained that I had founded a treatment that resets muscle memory after it becomes blocked due to emotional stress.

He could connect with my work, as he was an arbitrator in business and brought people together to resolve conflict. The one factor that linked all three treatments together was the death of the girls' brothers and sons from the same family. The girls had lost their last brother only six months prior to seeing me and the first brother 12 months before that. Unknown to the family, a very rare genetic disease lay dormant in their genes and the first brother showed symptoms when he was 34. He was diagnosed within weeks of this rare condition and passed away six months later.

Three months prior to his death, his younger brother displayed the same symptoms and was diagnosed with the same genetic disorder. He passed away November 2015. This double tragedy hit the family like a tsunami. It's hard enough dealing with one loss, let alone two losses, in such a close space of time. How can you turn such emotions of anger, bitterness, unfairness, fear, hate and deep pain into a celebration? The simple answer is you can't at first. Your mind and body go into shock and the bereavement process begins. Whilst you go through this free fall of emotions, you experience multiple levels of negative pain, both physically and mentally. You suffer tiredness, aches and pains, sleepless nights, dysfunction of the brain, headaches, sickness, loose bowels, back pain, moodiness, poor concentration and lack of motivation.

The only solution for many is to see the doctor, when you can't cope with these awful symptoms any more. Antidepressants are often prescribed to combat such dark days. For some people they help, but not for others. But what other way is there in dealing with it? If you search the internet there are lots of natural ways to help support your mind and body when such sad loss affects you.

Another client of mine was the most delightful woman you could ever wish to meet. In the short time I treated her, I was inspired by her wisdom, kindness, but most of all her humour. Sadly she lost her battle with cancer this year, at the young age of 69. Her wonderful daughter, Amy Hackett-Jones, a motivational life and leadership coach, turned her broken heart into a celebration of her mother's life. Even though a part of her had died inside, she owed it to her mother's memory to be the best person she could be, as a living testimony of all that her mother had taught her.

She lives each day of her life with meditation, mindfulness, lots of gratitude and of course, she counts her blessings. She knows that it still hurts inside, like a stab wound that never really heals. She takes comfort in positive memories of her mother through daily meditation. She is comforted by her walks in her mother's beloved rose garden, (her mother's favourite place at their home in Glenham Hall, Suffolk), and she knows that one day, she will be reunited with her mum.

Grieving is a personal and highly individual experience. How you grieve depends on many factors, including your personality and coping style, your life experience, your faith and the nature of the loss. The grieving process takes time. Healing happens gradually;

it can't be forced or hurried and there is no "normal" timetable for grieving. Some people start to feel better in weeks or months. For others, the grieving process is measured in years. Whatever your grief experience, it's important to be patient with yourself and allow the process to naturally unfold.

We all learn from each other in life and in death. Death just reminds you not to take people and your own life for granted. When a loved one passes, it's easy to lash out in grief and torment yourself. It's normal and part of the bereavement process. At the same time, it's not disrespectful to laugh at happy memories of times spent together and the joy they brought to every occasion you shared.

That's why it's so important to live each day as if it's your last, speaking to those people who mean so much to you in the best way you can. Most of my clients' physical pain is as a result of unresolved issues with their loved ones. Families have the biggest fallouts and feuds, but nothing gets resolved, even at the point of death. It's all about control, power and who's dictating who.

Learning to live your days to the fullest with no regrets means you have been the best person you can be, to everyone including yourself. If you left this planet, right now, would you be well remembered and missed? Your 50s and 60s are a great time to value and remember all this, so you still have time to change your outlook. If you're past 50/60 and reading this, that's fine too. It's never too late to change, for the good of you and others. It will always have a positive impact.

SUMMARY OF WHAT YOU HAVE LEARNED FROM THIS CHAPTER

- **Fact**: Time matters - make it every day count.
- **Fact**: Signs of ageing on the face and body is unavoidable. Decide what makes you happy entering the ageing process naturally or with a little help from surgery, either way it's your choice so enjoy the ride.

- **Fact**: Menopause is unavoidable and comes with many symptoms be prepared.

- **Fact**: Diet matters more acidic foods and drink will increase inflammation in the body leading to daily aches, pains.

- **Fact**: Physical pain increases with worry or stress due to increased production of adrenaline and cortisol in the body, you will ache more.

- **Fact**: Weight gain puts added pressure on your organs and joints creating more pain.

- **Fact**: Grieve may be experienced more frequent now as partners, family and friends pass away in your latter years.

WHAT YOU CAN DO RIGHT NOW TO CHANGE THINGS FOR THE BETTER

- Value your time - taking small noticeable daily moments for yourself, even if it's just to sit 5 minutes in your garden listening to the birds, it all counts towards your wellbeing.

- If you fear the physical changes, research in what way will you feel better about approaching your senior years, looking glamorous and forever young or accepting your wrinkles and fine lines gracefully is part of the process. Don't feel guilty about what other people think or say, just put yourself first.

- If you get menopause symptoms, address them quickly so you don't suffer in silence. Visit your GP or therapist for the necessary medication.

- You need to reduce or avoid stress in your daily life in order to reduce feeling pain in your body. Unnecessary worry no matter how small will add to it, it doesn't have to be a big stress. You need to be more mindful where your negative thinking will lead and what it will create. Try to look at difficult situations in a calmer frame of mind or even walk away till you feel calmer to address the situation.

- Start looking at your daily diet and increase your water intake. Eat more alkalising foods which will reduce inflammation and pain.

- Try to keep your body weight within your BMI as it is proven to reduce the impact of pressure on your joints and ligaments, to avoid pain.

- If you suffer a series of close deaths amongst family or friends, try to focus on the best memories you have of that person. Celebrate their life by doing something purposeful that adds meaning to yours. Get help and support from charities such as Cruse that specialise in helping people through the process.

BIG DECISIONS

THE GOLDEN YEARS - YOUR 70s, 80s, 90s

"You are never too old to set a new goal or dream a new dream"

~ C. S. Lewis ~

It's easy to think that the time has passed you by and it's too late to set a new goal or have a new dream. Maybe you've reached some of your goals and now you seem like you're just coasting along. Or maybe you think you're too old to get started on some great work. This is a quote for those who feel they're past the point of starting up anything new. It should spark a new fire and get you dreaming and goal-setting again. Always have a goal and a dream to pursue, as this is when you're at your happiest. As you get older your health may change and with it your needs. Being prepared can help you stay healthier for longer. Understanding and dealing with changes in your health, getting the right care and knowing your rights when you do need help will help you in your golden years. Looking after your mental and physical health can help you live well and stay happy, active and safe in later life.

This final chapter about age and pain through the decades is intended as an inspiration for everyone. There are lots of damaging things in the world today, on social media and on your doorstep, to send you to an early grave. It's true the last few decades could bring you heart disease, arthritis, dementia, Parkinson's disease and stroke, but the emphasis here is on the word COULD.

I am a realist and an optimist. I've survived a head-on collision, learned to walk again and fought my way back from chronic illness. I've nursed both my parents through sickness and old age. I've dealt with mental health, multiple challenges and I am still here, looking forward to the next few decades with gusto. We are all individuals; we know for certain we all have to 'time out' at some point. We know we may struggle with health issues, some of which will depend on our genetics, attitude and how good we've looked after ourselves over the years.

Keep Smiling

If I gave you a choice of either sitting in the cold, harsh rain with barely a blanket wrapped around you, or offer you a recliner to bathe yourself in the comfort of the warm sunshine, which would you choose? I know for me, that feeling the sunshine on my face is so much nicer. Choosing more sunshine in your life, to be an optimist, is like wearing an unbroken smile on the inside. It's to embrace life no matter what is thrown at you and don't think for one minute, just because you are getting older, life will get easier.

For many it doesn't get easier, but they have found a way to cope better and use their knowledge, experience, wisdom to look at life through a soft focus lens, rather than being caught up in the harsh reality. This isn't the same as looking at life through rose-tinted glasses. You've come too far by now and had enough knocks to know that life can be and is cruel at times. There will always be two sides to the story, two ways of looking at an argument. You just need to decide which side of the fence you prefer to be stood by - the optimistic or the pessimistic, good or bad, winner or loser. Whichever you choose will be the right one for you and no one can tell you otherwise. It will be based on what the majority of your life has been about, your personal battles, your work, your family challenges and your state of health.

So what can we look forward to in our latter years? Most people may by now be challenged by physical or mental health conditions. Even though I'm not there yet, I've looked and studied these age groups and have found two types - those who are self-motivated, interactive, sociable and possibly still working, and those who are negative, dependant on others, have little interest in any interaction, choosing to focus on their pill tray and medical needs.

You can't control what Mother Nature hands out. If your family has a history of arthritis, you might develop it in your lifetime. However, as people are now living longer, it pays to be good to your body. To exercise and eat a healthful diet will help you age, wherever possible, disease-free. Having a body mass index less than 25 will lower your risk for heart disease, diabetes, and cancer. You can't eat and drink the way you did in your 20s and 30s without repercussions on your body, but having a little of what you fancy always does you good. Moderation is key. As you age, if you listen and watch your body as it alters, you can decide if you want to stay your new increased size or make a difference and keep a healthy weight.

At some point it happens to everyone, yet we don't like that belly fat or slack skin emerging, but you can control it, if you want to. Most people believe that it's part of the ageing process, so accept these physical and mental changes. But some people never look their age and they are well in to their 80s or 90s. I am a strong believer that you can truly hold back growing older, by taking more care of yourself. If most people look back, they will have spent their time taking care of other people, partners, parents, children, pets, home and their job.

How much you invested in yourself, in your past decades, will reflect on how well you cope in your more senior years. My mother dedicated most of her life to serving others and thought very little of herself, which resulted in her suffering so much chronic physical and emotional pain from her 70s onwards. Through watching her live a lifetime of pain, I have learned that if I do not incorporate some regular, quality, element of daily me time, that actually makes a significant difference to my mental state, I can look forward to my latter years with some physical issues for sure.

The Science that Backs the Positive Mind

In the last five years, hundreds of academic papers have been published, studying the health effects of a positive attitude, which researchers call "dispositional optimism". They've linked this positive outlook on life to everything from decreased feelings of loneliness to increased pain tolerance.

Oddly enough, three decades ago, the outlook for research on optimism didn't look very good. But then, in 1985, Michael F. Scheier and Charles S. Carver published their seminal study, Optimism, Coping, and Health: Assessment and Implications of Generalised Outcome Expectancies in Health Psychology.

Researchers immediately embraced the simple hopefulness test they included in the paper and their work has now been cited in at least 3,145 other published works. Just as importantly, by testing the effect of a personality variable on a person's physical health, Scheier and Carver helped bridge the gap between the worlds of psychology and biology. After the paper, scientists had a method for seriously studying the healing powers of positive thinking.

Scheier and Carver's influential work shows how their humble study on human motivation inspired studies on mind-body interactions. Their optimism scale was an instant hit in the scientific community, increasing our understanding of the effects optimism has on the mind and body.

More continued research has been done since this study was first published. Most researchers have examined the relationship of optimism and well-being. This research shows how optimism is clearly associated with better psychological health, as seen through lower levels of depressed mood, anxiety, and general distress, when facing difficult life circumstances, including recovering from illness and disease.

A smaller, but still substantial, amount of research has studied associations with physical well-being. Most researchers at this point would agree that optimism is connected to positive physical health outcomes, including decreases in the likelihood of re-hospitalisation following surgery, the risk of developing heart disease, and mortality.

The study showed why optimists do better than pessimists. The answer is in the different coping strategies they use. Optimists are not simply being do-gooders. They're problem solvers who try to improve the situation. If it can't be altered, they're also more likely than pessimists to accept that reality and move on. Physically, they're more likely to engage in behaviours that help protect against disease and promote recovery from illness. They're less likely to smoke, drink and have poor diets, and they're more likely to exercise, sleep well and stick to rehab programs.

Pessimists, on the other hand, tend to deny, avoid and distort the problems they confront, and dwell on their negative feelings, blaming everyone, but themselves. It's easy to see now why pessimists don't do so well compared to optimists. Where does the optimism or pessimism come from? Many say it's based from childhood beliefs and ongoing life experience.

Positive thinking doesn't mean that you keep your head in the sand and ignore life's less pleasant situations. Positive thinking just means that you approach unpleasantness in a more positive and productive way. You think the best is going to happen, not the worst. Positive thinking often starts with self-talk. Self-talk is the endless stream of unspoken thoughts that run through your head. These automatic thoughts can be positive or negative. Some of your self-talk comes from logic and reason. Other self-talk may arise from misconceptions that you create because of lack of information. If the thoughts that run through your head are mostly negative, your outlook on life is more likely pessimistic.

If your thoughts are mostly positive, you're likely to be an optimist, someone who practises positive thinking. Negative thinking creates more physical pain, due to the over production of adrenaline. Your body has been in a physical battle most of your decades. The younger you are, the more resilient your body is to stress. But over the years it will have had an impact. Stress throughout your life has a positive effect when used correctly, but most of the time, we have allowed it to generate a build-up of lactic acid, that has been retained in the muscles, leading to wear and tear.

On 4th March 2014, researchers from the Mayo Clinic published their findings to explore the effects of positive thinking and optimism on health. Benefits include:

- An increased life span
- Lower rates of depression
- Lower levels of distress
- Greater resistance to the common cold
- Better psychological and physical well-being
- A reduced risk of death from cardiovascular disease
- Better coping skills during hardships and times of stress

You're Never Too Old. People Have Achieved Great Things When Society Said They Were Past it.

There is a myth that people believe, when you're past a certain age, you're past it. In Yorkshire, where I live, they say you're ready for the knacker's yard. This means that you are incapable of living life to the full, or not able to do what you once did, due to your failing years. I feel this to be an extremely insulting and disrespectful remark made against the elderly. It's discriminating against age.

Today's modern 20-somethings think you're past it when you're 40. At almost 53, I must be ancient! So let's look at some great achievements from well-known and ordinary people who challenged this myth.

- The oldest person to pass a driving test is the late Lord Renton, a Tory peer and former minister, who did so shortly before his 95th birthday in 2003. He'd actually been driving since the early 1930s but back then there was no formal driving test. Older drivers face no restrictions apart from being obliged to renew their licence every three years after their 70th birthday.
- The oldest male and female Oscar winners are Jessica Tandy,

at the age of 80, and Christopher Plummer, aged 82. Jessica, a British-American stage and film actress, enjoyed a 67-year career before her death in 1994. She appeared in more than 100 stage productions and had more than 60 roles in film and TV. She won her Oscar for 1989's Driving Miss Daisy for which she also received a BAFTA and a Golden Globe. Christopher Plummer made his film debut in 1958's Stage Struck. The Canadian is probably best known as widower Captain Von Trapp, who sings Edelweiss in the hit 1965 musical film The Sound of Music. He won numerous awards over his seven-decade career, but his first Oscar came for Best Supporting Actor in, ironically, Beginners in 2012.

- The oldest person to become Prime Minister was Lord Palmerston at the age of 71. Born in 1784, he entered the House of Commons at the age of 23. For 20 years he was a junior minister in a Tory government before changing parties, becoming the most successful Whig Foreign Secretary and Prime Minister in 1855. Serving twice as PM, he was the most recent to die whilst in office. After catching a chill that led to a violent fever he passed away, aged 80, in 1865. Palmerston was only the fourth non-royal to be given a state funeral, after Sir Isaac Newton, Lord Nelson and the Duke of Wellington.

- With temperatures plummeting to −43 °C the North Pole is a tough environment for anyone. But Dorothy Davenhill Hirsch, 89, became the oldest person to visit, aboard the Russian Nuclear Ice Breaker Yamal in 2004.

- Singer Dame Vera Lynn made British chart history in 2014 by becoming the oldest living artist to reach the Top 20 at the age of 97. The Forces' Sweetheart, who celebrated her 99th birthday in March this year, entered the UK's Official Albums Chart at number 13 with Vera Lynn: National Treasure and then went to number one.

- Wisdom comes with age and Dr Leila Denmark certainly had both on her side. The American paediatrician was still working until her retirement on May 2001 at the age of 103. She was also a super centenarian, living to be 114 years old.

- Former Mau Mau fighter Kimani Maruge, wanted an education. He enrolled in the first year at the age of 84 on January 12, 2004. He said the Kenyan government's announcement of universal and free elementary education in 2003 prompted him to learn to read. And he didn't stop there. In 2005 Maruge was elected head boy.
- The oldest woman to complete a marathon was Gladys Burrill from Hawaii, who was 92 years old. She power walked and jogged the Honolulu Marathon in nine hours 53 minutes, earning herself the nickname "Gladyator". She had run her first marathon aged 86.
- Retired Lt Col James C Warren is a former navigator of the Tuskegee Airmen, the first African American military aviators in the United States armed forces. At the ripe old age of 87 he became the world's oldest person to receive his pilot's licence.
- An 80-year old Japanese mountaineer reached the summit of Mount Everest in 2013 and incredibly this was after having had heart surgery. Yuichiro Miura first climbed Everest when he was 70 and then again at 75. After his last climb he said: "I think three times is enough". In 1970, while still a youngster, Miura skied down Everest, using a parachute to slow his descent. He is now planning to return on his 90th birthday.
- Bertha Wood, born in 1905, had her first book, 'Fresh Air and Fun: The Story of a Blackpool Holiday Camp' published on her 100th birthday on June 20, 2005. The book is based on her memoirs, which she began writing at the age of 90.
- John Glenn made history when, at the age of 77, he became the oldest person to travel in space. Born on July 18, 1921, the American had been a pilot and a US senator when he was selected for the Mercury Seven – the elite Military test pilots picked by NASA to operate the Mercury spacecraft and become the first US astronauts.
- At 96, South African Mohr Keet became the oldest bungee jumper ever. Disproving any myth that you become more fearful as you get older, he jumped from South Africa's Western Cape, which has a 708ft drop. It was his fifth jump

and the pensioner also admitted to enjoying white water rafting and parachuting.

- At 66, Elizabeth Adeney from Suffolk became Britain's oldest mum when she gave birth to a son in 2009. She had undergone IVF treatment in Ukraine.
- Carole Hobson from Kent will be 65 this month – but on Christmas Eve 2010 became Britain's oldest mother of twins. Freida and Matthew were conceived using donor embryos at an Indian clinic following four failed IVF attempts.
- The oldest mum in the world is Rajo Devi Lohan who gave birth in 2008 aged 69. The Indian fell pregnant following IVF treatment.

Evidence of Living to 100

"If you don't prioritise yourself, you constantly start falling lower and lower on your list" Michelle Obama

There are hundreds of people around the world celebrating becoming centenarians, probably due to better housing, safer jobs and improving medical care. Official figures from The Office of National Statistics (ONS) show the number of centenarians has quadrupled over the last 30 years. In 2014 there were 14,450 centenarians living in the UK including 780 over the age of 105, a record high. The ONS says a growing awareness of the importance of diet and exercise has also contributed to the rise.

More people are set to reach their centenary in the next few years with 550,810 Britons already aged 90 and over, almost three times the 187,250 in 1984. The number of centenarians living in the UK has risen by 6,030 – a 72 per cent jump in the last decade alone.

George Holley-Moore, research officer at the International Longevity Centre UK, welcomed the jump in numbers. He said: "The number of people living to 100 and over is obviously great news. Advances in healthcare means a group of the population which even ten years ago was relatively small has increased dramatically. Improvements in medical treatments for conditions such as cancer and heart disease has played an important role, but other factors such as improved nutrition and better housing conditions have also contributed".

Historical factors also come into play. The large increase in births after the First World War meant that there is a bigger pool of people to live into their 90s than in previous years. The post second world war baby boom will most probably have a similar impact in the future. The gap is closing primarily because of medical progress and lifestyle changes, including declining smoking rates in men and the closure of heavy industry, where more men than women worked in dangerous or dirty jobs.

The ONS explained: "Together these two major events contribute to the rises in women relative to men at age 90 and over in the 1980s and at age 100 and over in the 1990s, despite greater improvement in male mortality, compared to female mortality at older ages over the whole period, as fewer men were alive to reach the oldest ages".

Janet Morrison, chief executive of older people's charity Independent Age, said: "We welcome these new figures revealing a spectacular increase in the number of people aged 100 or over".

It's a remarkable fact that there is such a high number of centenarians in the UK, highlighting the significant progress we have made, particularly in medical care and public health over the last half century. Yet the UK remains unprepared for ageing in many crucial areas. The charity points out that the NHS, social care, transport and housing all require much more work if we are to successfully meet the needs of our rapidly ageing population.

The risk increases for lonely older people, living alone without support, company or friendship. These critical issues have been raised in the new 2030 Vision report, which warns politicians that there is no excuse for inaction and that they must act now to help society get ready for ageing.

Although centenarians account for only three per cent of the population aged 90 and over and just 0.02 per cent of the overall UK population, their numbers are growing. Overall England and Wales have more centenarians per 100,000 populations in 2014 than Scotland or Northern Ireland. In 1984, just 120 centenarians people were aged 105 or over but by 1994 the number had more than doubled to 280. By 2014, that number had soared by more than four times as many as the estimate of 3,250 30 years ago.

The Queen reached her own 90th birthday this year; however, she will be spending more and more time writing birthday cards to centenarians. At present, she sends a personal congratulatory message to anyone in the United Kingdom celebrating their 100th birthday, their 105th birthday, and each year following. Around the world, there were 450,000 people over the age of 100, according to the UN. The vast majority are women - accounting for 335,000 to just 89,000 men. Japan has the highest number of centenarians per 100,000 people anywhere in the world, with 47. By contrast the UK has only 22, well behind France which has the highest ratio in Europe at 34. Eastern European countries have the lowest proportions of centenarians within Europe

Be Inspired

Whether you've reached your golden years or not, there is so much to look forward to. Embrace the new world of technology and become more interactive with things you always wanted to do, but never made time for. We all have our inner child to satisfy and we still need to play, no matter what our age. A dear friend of the family who is now in her late 70s always loved computers, but never had the opportunity in her youth, due to other responsibilities, to study computing.

She decided when her husband, whom she was married to for 50 years, passed away, to enrol on an IT course at her local college. She learned how to send emails to her family around the world, how to do power point, create word documents and use Office. This gave her a new-found confidence and a chance to work part time to support a local charity in their office, doing admin work.

Instead of sitting at home, in the silence, feeling depressed due to her loss, she now feels that she is not only contributing to helping others, but she has been blessed with a second lease of life.

If you have your health or even if it is a challenge, there is nothing to stop you moving forward and making the best out of any situation. Here are more amazing people who started doing new things in their lives:

- Believed to have been the world's oldest blogger, Australian woman Olive Riley began her blog The Life of Riley in February 2007 at the age of 107 and made her final post on 26 June 2008 from a nursing home in Woy Woy, New South Wales, complaining of a cough about two weeks before she died at the age of 108. She had posted over 70 entries, as well as several video posts on YouTube. Her blog (or "blob" as she called it) was inspired by her experience with documentary filmmaker Michael Rubbo who, in 2005, made a documentary about her titled All About Olive.
- Winifred Pristell is a 70-year-old, competitive weightlifter with two world records and aspirations for more. Winifred first took up the sport in her late 40s due to her struggles with her weight. When she turned 60 she started to lift competitively in powerlifting meets. At 68, she set world records for her age in the bench press at 176.2 pounds and 270 pounds in the deadlift. Even though she has been struggling lately with arthritis and joint issues, at 70 Winifred still works out three days a week. She says she doesn't let her condition stop her. In fact, when she works out, she doesn't suffer any pain.
- Ron Cunningham, who died in 2007 at the age of 92, was the oldest escapologist and end-of the-pier artist specialising in feats such as eating light bulbs and removing a straitjacket while hanging upside down with his trousers on fire. To impress audiences, he put himself in great danger during many of his stunts using fire, water and glass at his local pub - the Bedford Tavern in Brighton. It was here where he performed his last stunt in 2005. This was the escape out

of handcuffs with both arms on fire with lighter fluid. He died in Brighton, East Sussex after a whisky and a cigar at his home on October 15, 2007. His last request was for a trapdoor in the hearse at his funeral. He wrote a short poem, which was read at the occasion: "They lay the Great Omani in his box. They have done it up with nails not locks. But at his funeral do not despair. Chances are he won't be there".

- A Los Angeles Metro employee for 72 years, Arthur Winston (1906 - 2006) was known for being honoured as the "Employee of the Century" because he was never late to work and only took one day off during his entire career - for his wife's funeral in 1988. He retired at age 100.

Active Celebrity Seniors

Over the years we have lost some of the most wonderful celebrities who have entertained us from around the world. They are part of our childhood and come from all walks of life. George Burns was an American comedian, actor, singer and writer. He smoked Cuban cigars from the age of 14 and passed away just after his 100th birthday of a heart attack. He worked up to the last five years of his life. It seems the more active you are in life, the longer you live. The more positive your approach to life is, the fewer health issues you have. The following celebrities living today, (at time of publication) all have this positive mindset:

- Clint Eastwood aged 86 years old, and still starring in and directing films. Born 31st May, 1930.
- Zsa Zsa Gabor is a Hungarian-American actress and socialite now 99 years of age. She is also famous for her nine husbands! Born 6th February, 1917
- Doris Day, a popular American actress, was known for The Doris Day Show. Aged 92. Born on 3rd April, 1924.
- Jimmy Carter was the 39th President of the United States. Aged 91. Born on 1st October, 1924.
- Franco Zeffirelli, an Italian director and producer, was known for his work on Romeo and Juliet (1968), Hamlet (1990). Aged 93. Born on 12th February, 1923.

- Stan Lee, an iconic American comic book writer and former chairman of Marvel Comics, aged 94. Born on 28th December, 1922.
- Prince Phillip, The Duke of Edinburgh, aged 95. Born on 10th June, 1921.
- Carol Channing, an American actress, singer, dancer, comedian and voice artist, aged 95. Born 31st January, 1921
- Billy Graham, the American Evangelist, who was ordained as a Southern Baptist minister, aged 97 still active. Born on 7th November, 1918.

SUMMARY OF WHAT YOU HAVE LEARNED FROM THIS CHAPTER

- **Fact**: Your mind matters - how you think will; affect how you physically feel.
- **Fact**: Optimistic people have fewer aches, pains or struggles in later life.
- **Fact**: People are globally living for longer thanks to better facilities, homes, food and health.
- **Fact**: There are more centenarians than ever before. Be inspired to become one of them.

WHAT YOU CAN DO RIGHT NOW TO CHANGE THINGS FOR THE BETTER

- Plan what you would still like to do, taking into consideration your financial circumstances and health. Even if you are caring for a partner or your grandchildren, you need to factor yourself into the equation.
- If it is a new venture, do your homework and research in depth so you know what will be expected of you.
- If you are struggling to be optimistic, because most of your life you've been pessimistic, engage the support of a professional person such as a therapist or a

psychologist, who can help you refocus. It is particularly good to have a neutral person, especially if your family, friends or partner are against your ideas.

- Our mind thinks that we are still 20, but our body tells us otherwise. Helping to retrain your body through gentle exercise, walking and gardening, which keeps us physically fit, will build muscle strength, allowing us to do more of what we want. Where there is a will, there is a way!
- Above all else - keep happy, keep strong, keep well!

9

THE POWER OF THE MIND

AND BRAIN CHANGES THROUGH THE DECADES

"The best way to forget the bad things in life is to learn to remember the good things"

~ Mark Amend ~

This is such a true sentence, but often people get it mixed around. Most often people will forget the good things and remember the bad things. Not only that, they'll want to focus on the bad things so much, explore them and wonder what they mean. This leads them down a dark path that has no ending.

Instead, they should just forget those bad things and only try to remember the good things, so more good things can come their way. The more you think about something, the more you get. The importance of our memory and our brain has always been a long fascination for me. During the years founding my treatment LT Therapy based on resetting muscle memory, I learnt the importance of the physical memory system in order for our body to move automatically. I also learned how important our memory is behind our behaviour.

Like the rest of your body, your brain changes with each passing year. From the time we are infants, our brains are adapting, learning, making memories and more. We become smarter and sharper, earning the wisdom that truly only comes with life experience. The less desirable effects of our memory can certainly be felt, too. You may recognise them in a lost set of keys, a To Do list that never seems to stay at the top of your mind, a name that's on the tip of your tongue.

Once we hit our late 20s, the brain's ageing process begins and we begin losing neurons, the cells that make up the brain and nervous system. By our 60s, our brains have literally begun to shrink. Though these brain changes may sound a bit scary, the process is natural and it happens to everyone. Learn how your brain changes as you age to get a better handle on what is happening in this magical part of your body. Then, review some of the things that you can do to help preserve brain health. Though some change is inevitable, some can be warded off with a healthy lifestyle.

How Our Brain Changes Through The Decades

Birth to Toddler Years

You are born with basic survival skills, reflexes and most of the 100 billion neurons that you'll have for the duration of your life. The brain grows incredibly rapidly during these early years. Neurons get bigger, work more efficiently and as a result of environmental input and stimuli, make trillions of connections that fine-tune everything from hearing to vision. By two years old, your brain is about 80 percent of its adult size.

Early to Middle Childhood

About 85 percent of brain development has occurred by now, including intellect, personality and motor and social skills. A child's brain has twice as many synapses as an adult's brain. In a process called pruning, the neural connections that are used and reinforced most often, like those used for language, are strengthened, while the ones that are not utilized as much, fizzle and die. (That's why parents are often encouraged to repeat certain activities, like reading books, with their kids every day).

Teens

At this point the brain reaches its adult weight of about three pounds. Increased activity in the frontal lobes allows a teenager to compare several concepts at once.

20s

The regions in the frontal lobe that are responsible for judgement, planning, weighing risks and decision-making finally finish developing. A twenty-something's brain has reached its peak in terms of performance.

Late 20s to Early 30s

Reasoning, spatial skills and speed of thought begin to decline around now. As you age, your brain goes through changes that can slow down your thinking. It loses volume, the cortex becomes thinner, the myelin sheath surrounding the fibres of your neurons begins to degrade, and your brain receptors don't fire as quickly.

Mid 30s

In your 30s, memory begins to slip as the number of neurons in the brain decreases. It may take longer to learn new things or memorise words or names. This process continues in the decades ahead.

40s and 50s

From your mid-40s to late 50s, your reasoning skills slow. In a group of people who were first tested on various mental abilities when they were 45-49 years old, reasoning skills declined by 3.6 percent over 10 years, according to research in the British Medical Journal. The middle-age participants also experienced fading sharpness in memory and verbal fluency, the ability to say words quickly in a specific category.

On the upside, other measures of cognition, such as moral decision-making, regulating emotions and reading social situations, have been shown to improve beginning with middle age. Experts suspect that simply living life and gaining experience deserves some of the credit. (Bonus fact: Starting at around age 40, people tend to remember positive images more than negative ones-a trend that continues until at least age 80.)

60s

The brain has begun to shrink in size and, after a lifetime of gaining accumulated knowledge, it becomes less efficient at accessing that knowledge and adding to it. The greatest risk factor for Alzheimer's is advancing age, and most individuals with the disease are 65 or older. Surprisingly, when Alzheimer's hits people in their 60s and 70s, they show faster rates of brain tissue loss and cognitive decline compared to patients 80 years and older, according to researchers at the University of California, San Diego School of Medicine. Researchers aren't sure why Alzheimer's is more aggressive in younger patients, but suspect that people who develop symptoms later in life may have milder cases or cases that take longer to reveal themselves.

70s and 80s

Your risk of developing Alzheimer's increases with age, reaching 50 percent by age 85. Researchers aren't sure why the risk jumps so dramatically as we get older, but it's possible the disease is linked to inflammation, a natural part of ageing that can lead to a build-up of deposits in areas like the hippocampus, the part of the brain responsible for forming new memories. These deposits may also interfere with long-term memory. Along with ageing, many experts think that genes and lifestyle contribute to the majority of Alzheimer's and dementia cases.

Proven Brain Boosters

Even the healthiest among us cannot stop our brains from changing with time. That being said, certain behaviours can help your brain stay as sharp as possible. Here's how you can take an active role in slowing negative effects and working to stay sharper longer.

- Break a Sweat. Exercise pumps blood to the brain and encourages the growth of new brain cells—and you don't have to spend hours at the gym to get the positive effects. Research shows that regular aerobic exercise, like walking or cycling, for 30 minutes a day reduces brain cell loss. (Regular physical activity can also significantly reduce the risk of heart attack, stroke, diabetes and more.)

- Challenge Yourself. Studies show that mentally stimulating activities may help reverse cognitive decline. Just as lifting dumbbells strengthens your muscles, keeping your mind engaged seems to increase the brain's vitality and may build its reserves of brain cells and connections. Do stimulating activities that you enjoy. Read, write, put together a jigsaw puzzle, do crosswords... it all counts.

- Listen to Music. A study in the journal Neuron showed that listening to music may sharpen the brain's ability to anticipate events and stay focused. Researchers took an MRI of people's brains while they were listening to symphony music, and then when they weren't. When music played, the areas of the brain involved with paying attention, making predictions and accessing memories were engaged; the same couldn't be said when it was quiet.

- Nurture Your Relationships. Invest in your bonds with friends and loved ones. Experts suspect that social interaction requires you to engage the areas of the brain involved in memory and attention, the same mental processes that are used in many cognitive tasks. Furthermore, one study revealed that activities that combine social interaction with physical and mental activity may help prevent dementia. Sign up for a dance class, which allows you to spend time with pals, get moving and challenge your brain as it works to keep up with all those tricky steps.

- Eat Wisely. Certain foods are rich in vitamins and other nutrients that can help thwart threats to your brain health. For example, regularly eating vibrantly coloured fruits and vegetables, which have high levels of disease-fighting antioxidants, will help counteract disease-causing free radicals throughout the body, including the brain. Cook meals with ingredients containing mono- and polyunsaturated fats, which can improve levels of HDL ("good") cholesterol and according to research, may help protect brain cells.

- Drink in Moderation. While we do not recommend taking up drinking alcoholic beverages, you might be surprised to learn that drinking alcohol sparingly may be beneficial to your brain. At least five studies have linked low-dose alcohol consumption, a drink a day for women, two for men, with a reduced risk of dementia in older adults. Be careful not to go outside those limits. Heavy alcohol use has been linked to an increased risk of dementia and cognitive decline.
- Stay Smoke Free. Smoking can affect your body's ability to deliver to the brain oxygen and nutrients that help keep it healthy and some studies have indicated that it can even speed up the brain's natural ageing process. Smoking can also lead to the formulation of plaques that can contribute to dementia.
- Protect Your Head. Experts think that there may be a connection between serious head injury and Alzheimer's disease, especially when trauma occurs repeatedly or involves loss of consciousness. Protect your brain by wearing a seatbelt, using a helmet when participating in sports and fall-proofing your home.

Dr Mary Newport is an author and a paediatric and neonatal specialist. Her husband Steve was diagnosed with Alzheimer's Disease in his mid-50s. She has a theory that ketone bodies, which the body makes when digesting coconut oil, may be an alternative fuel for the brain. She believes that coconut oil may offer profound benefits in the fight against Alzheimer's Disease. If her theory is accurate, it could be one of the greatest natural health discoveries in years.

Dr Newport has her own personal history with Alzheimer's. Her husband, Steve, suffered from progressive dementia for at least five years in his mid-50s, then had an MRI that supported a clinical diagnosis of Alzheimer's Disease. She recounts her story in a case study.

"Many days, often for several days in a row, he was in a fog; couldn't find a spoon or remember how to get water out of the refrigerator.

One day I would ask if a certain call came that I was expecting and he would say 'No.' Two days later he would remember the message from so-and-so from a couple of days earlier and what they said".

Dr Newport noted that her husband had no short-term memory, yet the information was still filed somewhere in his brain. She had a gut feeling that his diet had something to do with it. He began taking medication in hopes that it would help slow the process, but he became depressed, lost weight, forgot how to cook, use a calculator or even perform simple addition. Steve forgot how to perform many common tasks, but would spend all day working in the yard or in his garage and remained in good physical condition.

A few studies about the potential use of medium chain triglycerides or ketone bodies to not only treat, but prevent Alzheimer's disease caught Dr Newport's eye. Medium chain triglycerides are also regarded as a potential treatment for Parkinson's disease, Huntington's disease, multiple sclerosis, drug-resistant epilepsy and diabetes. Dr Newport explains: "Ketone bodies may help the brain recover after a loss of oxygen in new-borns through adults, may help the heart recover after an acute attack, and may shrink cancerous tumours. Children with drug resistant epilepsy sometimes respond to an extremely low carbohydrate ketogenic diet".

The body's cells may be able to use ketone bodies as an alternative fuel when glucose is unavailable. Ketone bodies do not normally circulate in the body unless it has been starving for a few days, or if one is on a very low-carb diet, such as Atkins. Dr Newport explains, "In Alzheimer's disease, the neurons in certain areas of the brain are unable to take in glucose due to insulin resistance and slowly die off. If these cells had access to ketone bodies, they could potentially stay alive and continue to function".

Dr Newport started giving a daily dose of coconut oil to her husband, Steve. Just 60 days after he started taking it, Dr Newport recalls that Steve was alert and happy, talkative and making jokes, and the tremor he'd developed was less noticeable. He was able to concentrate on one task instead of being easily distracted. Steve receives about 2 tablespoons of coconut oil twice a day, to make sure that there are no periods where ketone bodies aren't circulating. After a year of the natural treatment, Dr Newport says her husband is a different person. She notes that he still has difficulty finding some words, but he recognised relatives on a family trip, participated actively in conversations, and his facial expressions were more animated.

She adds: "For now, we are very pleased with where he is at and should coconut oil stop or slow down the progress of his disease, it will be worth every drop that he takes".

Her exciting work in this field is currently being closely monitored by consultants specialising in Alzheimer's and dementia worldwide.

Diet and Brain Health

Dementia UK shows that recent studies have concluded that the MIND diet (Mediterranean-DASH Intervention for Neurodegenerative Delay) can aid brain health. It is a combination of a diet to reduce blood pressure (DASH) and the Mediterranean diet.

10 "Brain Healthy" Foods

- Green leafy veg
- Other colourful veg
- Nuts
- Berries – e.g. blueberries, strawberries
- Beans, lentils, soya
- Fish
- Poultry
- Olive oil
- Red wine – in moderation!
- Wholegrains

5 "Unhealthy" Foods

- Red meats
- Butter and margarines

- Cheese
- Pastries and sweets
- Fried and "fast foods"

Exercise and the Ageing Brain

If certain foods and eating a colourful diet aids the brain, then exercise can have the same effect. A paper published in Science Direct in October 2002 showed while limited research is available, physical and mental activity influence the ageing process. Human data show functions of the type associated with frontal lobe and hippocampal regions of the brain may be maintained or enhanced in humans with higher levels of fitness. Exercise increases blood flow to the brain, delivering the nutrition it needs to fully function.

The Power of the Mind -Scientific Proof That Negative Beliefs Harm Your Health

The medical establishment has been proving that the mind can heal the body for over 50 years. We call it "the placebo effect," and we know that when patients in clinical trials get nothing, but sugar pills, saline injections or fake surgeries, but believe they might be getting the new wonder drug or miracle surgery, their bodies get better 18 to 80% of the time.

While many are aware of the seemingly mysterious placebo effect, fewer people know about its evil twin, "the nocebo effect". Dr Lissa Rankin M.D author of Mind Over Medicine: Scientific Proof That You Can heal Yourself, became convinced that a combination of positive belief and the nurturing care of the right healer can activate the body's natural self-repair mechanisms and help the body heal itself.

I agree with her findings. When I work on a client to reset their muscle memory, I am doing just that. I am connecting their physical pain with their unconscious mind. Using LT Therapy, I identify what negative memory they are revisiting, that continually creates their physical pain. But do negative beliefs about our health or harsh care from insensitive doctors harm the body? Yes, they can.

Harmful Beliefs Poison Your Body

As reported in an article in The Lancet, researchers in San Diego examined the death records of almost 30,000 Chinese-Americans and compared them to over 400,000 randomly selected white people. What they found was that Chinese-Americans, but not whites, die significantly earlier than normal (by as much as five years) if they have a combination of disease and were born in a year considered bad luck in Chinese astrology and Chinese medicine!

The researchers found that the more strongly the Chinese-Americans attached to traditional Chinese superstitions, which they believe to be true, the earlier they died. When they examined the data, they concluded that the reduction in life expectancy could not be explained by genetic factors, the lifestyle choices or behaviour of the patients, the skill of the doctors, or any other variable.

Why did the Chinese-Americans Die Younger?

The researchers concluded that they died younger not because they have Chinese genes, but because they have Chinese beliefs. They believe they will die younger because the stars have told them. Their negative beliefs manifested as a shorter life span.

It's not just Chinese Americans whose fears about their health can result in negative health outcomes. One study showed that 79% of medical students report developing symptoms suggestive of the illnesses they are studying. They get paranoid and think they'll get sick; their bodies comply by getting sick. I know this to be true from my own personal experience, which I shared in my second book, when I fell ill after my parents' acrimonious divorce.

You Can Think Yourself Sick

Whether you're a Chinese-American, a medical student, or someone like Angelina Jolie, who may have been medically cursed with a poor prognosis. You may be at high risk of disease or death, or even just someone whose subconscious mind is filled with limiting beliefs from your childhood like "I'm the often-get-ill type", or "My family gets cancer". Focusing your attention on illness has been scientifically proven to predispose the body to illness. Excessive knowledge about what can go wrong with the body can actually harm you. The more you focus on the infinite ways in which the body can break down, the more likely you are to experience physical symptoms.

While the placebo effect demonstrates the power of positive thinking, expectation, hope, and nurturing care, the nocebo effect demonstrates the physiological effects of negative belief, fear, anxiety, and what American psychologist and self-help author Martin Seligman terms "learned helplessness". These negative emotions trigger the amygdala in the limbic brain to send out a red alert that activates the "fight-or-flight" stress response. When the nervous system is in "fight-or-flight", the body's self-repair mechanisms don't function properly and the body is predisposed to illness. All because you thought yourself sick. The same with pain, the more you focus on your pain, the more it becomes established, and the longer you will feel it.

How Long Do You Believe You'll Live?

The good news is that by changing your thoughts, you can change your health! Becca Levy, professor of Psychology and leading researcher in the fields of social gerontology and psychology of ageing, studied how our beliefs about longevity affect how long we live. What did she find? Those who lived longest were those who believed they would live the longest.

Dr Bernie Siegel, author of Love, Medicine and Miracles and one of the Professors in the MD training programme at the Whole Health Medicine Institute founded by Dr Lissa Rankin, asked Lissa how long she intended to live. She said: "A hundred years." He replied: "Good answer, because what you believe will come true". I can relate to this, as I have always asked myself this question and I always get the same reply - 103.

I'm not suggesting that positive belief is the only factor. Obviously, accidents happen, genetic risk factors influence our health and bad things happen to good people with positive thoughts. But the studies show that, even in light of these things we can't always prevent, what we believe, especially what we fear, has a tendency to manifest itself in reality because negative beliefs fill our bodies with harmful cortisol and epinephrine, while positive beliefs relax our nervous systems and allow our bodies to heal.

You are the Gatekeeper of Your Mind

You wouldn't take a pill from a bottle with a skull and crossbones on it, but every time you think negative thoughts about your health, you're potentially poisoning your body with stress hormones, that deactivate your body's natural self-repair mechanisms. You are the gatekeeper of your mind, and it's your responsibility to protect what you think. What thoughts do you choose to think about your body?

Our Second Brain

When you are stressed, your gut knows it, immediately. The enteric nervous system is often referred to as our body's second brain. There are hundreds of millions of neurons connecting the brain to the enteric nervous system, the part of the nervous system that is tasked with controlling the gastrointestinal system. A primal connection exists between our brain and our gut. We often talk about a "gut feeling" when we meet someone for the first time. We're told to "trust our gut instinct" when making a difficult decision. This mind-gut connection is not just metaphorical.

Our brain and gut are connected by an extensive network of neurons and a highway of chemicals and hormones that constantly provide feedback about how hungry we are, whether or not we're experiencing stress, or if we've ingested a disease-causing microbe. This information superhighway is called the brain-gut axis and it provides constant updates on the state of affairs at your two ends.

This vast web of connections monitors the entire digestive tract from the oesophagus to the anus. The enteric nervous system is so extensive that it can operate as an independent entity, without input from our central nervous system, although they are in regular communication. While our "second" brain cannot compose a symphony or paint a masterpiece, the way the brain in our skull can, it does perform an important role in managing the workings of our inner tube. The network of neurons in the gut is as plentiful and complex as the network of neurons in our spinal cord, which may seem overly complex just to keep track of digestion. Why is our gut the only organ in our body that needs its own "brain"? Is it just to manage the process of digestion? Or could it be that one job of our second brain is to listen in on the trillions of microbes residing in the gut? Just like your muscle memory listens in on your inner thinking.

Operations of the enteric nervous system are overseen by the brain and central nervous system. The central nervous system is in communication with the gut via the sympathetic and parasympathetic branches of the autonomic nervous system, the involuntary arm of the nervous system that controls heart rate, breathing and digestion. The autonomic nervous system is tasked with the job of regulating the speed at which food transits through the gut, the secretion of acid in our stomach and the production of mucus on the intestinal lining. The hypothalamic-pituitary-adrenal axis, or HPA axis, is another mechanism by which the brain can communicate with the gut to help control digestion through the action of hormones.

This circuitry of neurons, hormones and chemical neurotransmitters not only sends messages to the brain about the status of our gut, it allows for the brain to directly impact the gut environment. The rate at which food is being moved and how much mucus is lining the gut, both of which can be controlled by the central nervous system have a direct impact on the environmental conditions the microbiota experiences.

Like any ecosystem inhabited by competing species, the environment within the gut dictates which inhabitants thrive. Just as creatures adapted to a moist rain forest would struggle in the desert, microbes relying on the mucus layer will struggle in a gut where mucus is exceedingly sparse and thin. Bulk up the mucus, and the mucus-adapted microbes can stage a comeback. The nervous system, through its ability to affect gut transit time and mucus secretion, can help dictate which microbes inhabit the gut. In this case, even if the decisions are not conscious, it's mind over microbes.

What about the microbial side? When the microbiota adjusts to a change in diet or to a stress-induced decrease in gut transit time, is the brain made aware of this modification? Does the brain-gut axis run in one direction only, with all signals going from brain to gut, or are some signals going the other way? Is that voice in your head that is asking for a snack coming from your mind or is it emanating from the insatiable masses in your bowels? Recent evidence indicates that not only is our brain "aware" of our gut microbes, but these bacteria can influence our perception of the world and alter our behaviour. It is becoming clear that the influence of our microbiota reaches far beyond the gut, to affect an aspect of our biology few would have predicted - our mind. In simple terms, the bacteria that colonises your gut can affect your mind.

You have learned that how you think not only affects how you feel mentally, but how your body responds physically. Your brain in the skull will affect your second brain in the gut, by the messages you are sending it unconsciously. By understanding this process, you can begin to influence important changes in your diet, by eating more clean foods (less sugar), more alkalising food in the form of fresh green vegetables, and less acidic meat.

To help the gut you need a good probiotic. As a garden needs good nutritious soil to feed its plants and encourage new growth, a daily probiotic will help to colonise the much-needed good bacteria that our more acidic diets kill. Healthy people who don't get stressed can get this from a yoghurt drink which has probiotics in it. However, people who live a more stressful life or are compromised by health issues will need a more professional formulation.

I take Optibac Probiotics which can be purchased on the internet or any good high street chemist. They specialise in formulations for various gut conditions and work really well. I know after having a severe bout of viral gastroenteritis two years ago, it killed all my good gut bacteria, so I had to recolonise quickly. They did the job. Taking a regular probiotic also helps boost your immune system and protects you from allergies. My hay fever has practically gone since I've been on them.

Probiotics help to maintain healthy levels of good bacteria in the intestines, they support our immune defences, are useful for anyone suffering from the uncomfortable symptoms of bloating, gas or flatulence and they may assist in decreasing the duration of diarrhoea in kids. They may also help to restore good bacteria after a course of antibiotics. Prebiotics are 'non-living' food ingredients that reach the large intestine, unaffected by digestion and 'feed' the good bacteria in our gut, helping them to grow and flourish. Having a combination of prebiotic and probiotic rich foods, and topping up with a supplement if needed, can help our bodies maintain a healthy balance of good bacteria and support mental health and wellbeing.

Foods Containing Natural Prebiotics

Legumes

- Wholewheat products
- Rye based foods
- Artichokes
- Onions
- Cabbage
- Garlic and
- Chicory root which contains inulin

Foods Containing Natural Probiotics

- Yogurt. One of the best probiotic foods is live-cultured yogurt, especially handmade

- Kefir. Similar to yogurt, this fermented dairy product is a unique combination of goat's milk and fermented kefir grains.
- Sauerkraut
- Dark chocolat
- Microalgae
- Miso soup
- Pickles
- Tempeh

If your diet does not contain pre or probiotics naturally every day, then take a supplement. This has also been known to be very helpful in reducing and controlling symptoms of IBS and Ulcerative Colitis.

SUMMARY OF WHAT YOU HAVE LEARNED FROM THIS CHAPTER

- **Fact**: Your Brain changes as you grow and get older
- **Fact**: Your diet (what you eat) and how you exercise (how you move) affects how your brain functions
- **Fact**: A positive thinking pattern will heal your mind and body, protecting you from pain and ill health
- **Fact**: A negative thinking pattern will harm you, triggering pain and illness in the mind and body
- **Fact**: The body has a second brain, The Enteric Nervous System, commonly called 'the second brain'

WHAT YOU CAN DO RIGHT NOW TO CHANGE THINGS FOR THE BETTER

- Feed your mind and body a balanced diet incorporating leafy green vegetables, oily fish, nuts, whole grains, with plenty of water daily. The brain is made of 80% water so ensuring you do not get dehydrated means you reduce fatigue and think more clearly.

- Feed your 'second brain' - your gut - with a daily pre and probiotic to boost your immune system and overall wellbeing
- Keep a positive and optimistic mind daily, guard and protect yourself from negative thoughts that are toxic and only serve to harm you

10
A LIFE WITHOUT PAIN
SIMPLE STEPS TO A PAIN-FREE MIND & BODY

"All our dreams can come true if we have the courage to pursue them"
~ Walt Disney ~

Disney infused many of his films with positive messages about achieving your dreams and what it takes to live a magical life. It's no wonder that he was able to achieve many of his dreams in his lifetime and leave a lasting legacy. Do you have the courage to pursue your dreams, and if so, what have you done lately that is moving you forward towards your dreams? Just remember that courage means feeling the fear and doing it anyway. Everything you want is on the other side of fear.

"Letting go gives us freedom, and freedom is the only condition for happiness" Thich Nhat Hanh

Thich Nhat Hanh refers to letting go of the emotional pain we keep inside our heads, the emotional memories that will bind you to your pain. Once you have healed those painful memories of the past or present day, you've earned your freedom to live a life free of pain. A pain-free mind is a pain-free body.

Our lives are fleeting, and the best day to fight for the right to live a full life, is today. You can't change yesterday (the past) and you cannot foresee tomorrow (the future) so why worry about something over which you've no control. Why waste valuable time and energy on doing something that will result only in pain? You might as well do something amazing today, and by "amazing", I mean, taking small, positive steps forward on a purposeful path.

Everything you want and need to do, in order to make a positive change for the better takes daily practice, something you won't always commit to because life gets in the way. You are being tested every day, with these small challenges, to see if you can put yourself first? Committing to doing something daily that heals you inside and out has to be your priority, if you want to eliminate pain in your life.

This is not about being selfish or opening up feelings of guilt, because you are giving yourself permission to spend some daily time on you. This is about you, understanding that, in order for you to stop suffering mentally and physically, you have to NOW invest in YOU, because you are worth being on this testing planet. You're the amazing person you always have been, but have never given yourself permission to be.

If you continue to be a workaholic, shopaholic or familyaholic (putting others first), you will eventually lose sight of the reason as to why you are here (which is not to always serve others) and even worse, who you are as a person. I see so many wonderful people who have just lost themselves in life's maze. They have been so busy pleasing their boss, family, partner, children, parents and friends that they forget to please themselves. When I ask them what they enjoy in life, what their hobbies and interests are, more than half say they don't know. They can't remember what they used to like and what gave them pleasure. That's their 'wake up' call to change.

In order to get out of this cycle of serving others, you need to do something daily that helps you to heal emotionally. Whether it means practising gratitude, mindfulness, meditation or sitting for 10 minutes and being still. Listen to your breath gently calming you inside, appreciating you in this moment and thanking you for taking this time to value you. This is a form of simple meditation which can be done anywhere. Particularly effective after stress, it helps calm your mind. You might decide to relax in a healing salt bath three times a week and stay there for 20 minutes. For some people this can be a challenge in itself.

Most people today want a quick shower, as they need to get on with their busy day. Taking a bath is a slow, time-consuming process that they just don't have time for. The irony is, you really need the bath because in that bath, your mind and body will relax and shut out all the interruptions you constantly get from your job, family, phone and emails. Bath time means me time. I dare you to do it and you can't take your phone with you! At first you'll want to get out as soon as you've got in, but as you force yourself to stay a few minutes longer, you are training your mind and body to come together and work as one.

For those people who already have lots of baths and can stay in for 30 minutes, forgive me; you get a star for mastering this relaxing process. I am addressing the novice bathers here. This is a luxury to be enjoyed, just as you did when you were a baby; even though you can't remember back then, your unconscious mind will. This is where your inner child lives; he or she needs their playtime in the bath. Please don't forget to include, if you wish, any bath toys like rubber ducks and boats. This is your bath time experience so make it fun and relaxing. Bath products have made a recent comeback in the shops. Bathing was seen as a significant ritual the Romans pleasured in, not just an important way to cleanse the body, but to find inner peace.

Walking in nature, your garden or in the park to appreciate the healing benefits of bird song, or simply people watching or looking for squirrels or hedgehogs is re-energising. Just sit and watch time pass, without needing to clock watch. You will allow yourself to stop time and enjoy the moment, to recharge your batteries.

In the film Pretty Woman, Julia Roberts makes Richard Gere do just this. He's a stressed-out executive with a major decision to make and he can't focus. She sees him constantly on his phone talking to his solicitors, trying to seal the deal, but he never does. She takes him to the park for the day, so he can disconnect from his busy business world. At first he finds it difficult to adjust to his new surroundings. He feels almost embarrassed, as she removes his socks and shoes, allowing his feet to feel the texture of the grass, letting him connect with nature again. Eventually, he succumbs to the wonderful feeling he gets from the peaceful surroundings. He is able to think more clearly, get focused and makes the right decision about the deal. Taking time out of your day for yourself allows you to get clarity about the direction towards which you're working, for your own inner healing and peace.

In life, we are all working towards something; that's why goals are so important. It is your life map to where you are heading, it's what makes you feel complete at the end of your journey.

If you feel isolated or lonely, have lost friends or your loved ones have moved on, then you may need to think about joining a club. Even if you've stopped yourself before, too afraid to go on your own, it's one of the main ways to meet other people with a similar interest. Learn to dance, cycle, run, bake, sing, garden, speak a foreign language or play an instrument. Whatever you choose will release the creative side of you, allowing you to play and have fun. In each of these tasks, it's the action or performance of a dedicated precise set of acts, mental and physical, from which you get a sense of achievement and satisfaction of the inner spirit.

Daily practice means to perform, over and over again, in the face of all obstacles, some act of vision, faith, or desire. It's the only means of lifelong fulfilment. When you do this on a continual loop, you begin to master how to become pain-free.

In my first book, I wrote about how you can become pain-free through a healthy daily diet and exercise plan. I focused on exercises that were easy to achieve every day. Adding more movement in your day, like walking, dancing or rebounding delivers real results. However, you are the controller of you, the captain of your mind and body, taking responsibility. To understand how much movement I was doing each day, I had to have something that I could see, to keep me on track. I have worn a pedometer on my wrist for the past two years to monitor how many steps I actually do each day. The results are quite shocking.

As a therapist, I am on my feet a minimum of 12 hours a day, but can frequently go up to 16 hours. On days like this, I average about 14,000 steps. As a writer when I'm sitting at my desk, studying and researching, I can sit for up to 10 hours a day, with a few breaks. On such days I only total 5,000 steps or fewer.

In order for anyone to prevent weight gain and maintain a healthy BMI, the government recommends we do 10,000 steps a day, which is about five miles. If you fall under this number, because your day job is more sedentary, then you have to take responsibility and move more. I know after sitting on your bum all day, you will be lacking motivation to move, but don't complain when you get on those scales and you are up by half a stone, or worse, your clothes become extremely tight. You have only yourself to blame.

This is not about apportioning blame; this is a wake-up call which I'm doing in a very loving way. I truly respect, value and care for everyone. I see people in my clinic who are suffering physically because they choose not to move more, or eat less. or even eat more healthily. Remember, I've been there so I know what a battle it can be, but I also know that you can conquer it as well. As much as you are the cause of your problems, you are also your solution.

I always gain weight when I'm writing a book due to a more sedentary work day, but to counteract that I should get on my mini trampoline and bounce towards my daily 10,000 steps, but on this occasion I didn't. Why? Because my rebounder (trampoline) had broken and I never got it repaired over the past six months, hence I managed to add an extra stone to my body weight over the last four months. See how easily it can be done; then if you add the extra calories from snacking or alcohol in the evening, which is extremely easy and dangerous, you have the perfect combination for weight gain and pain.

Physical pain is not just caused by conditions we are predisposed to, it's not just caused because you get to a certain age and you have to accept it. It's caused by lifestyle choices; decisions you make every day. I told you before, you are only human and you will be affected by your emotions. Emotions play a huge part in how you eat every day. The more stressed you feel, the more ready-made meals, processed and sugary foods you will go for. You are programmed to go for them; you are addicted to them. Breaking bad eating habits is challenging, I know this so well, but when I put myself there and decide it is now time for change, my most important ally is my brain (what I tell myself) in whether I succeed or fail.

You have to become self-motivated to be fit and fight the flab. If you can't do it on your own, you will need to choose a support group or someone who can keep you on task. That's why Slimming World and Weight Watchers are two of the top national support groups for losing weight. When you have an off day, do not talk negative to yourself or you will continue the destructive pattern and fail. Accept it's just been one of those days and tomorrow, as Vivien Leigh said in Gone with the Wind, is another day. You've learned in earlier chapters of this book, that carrying extra weight is one of the main reasons you suffer physical pain.

The second is a poor mental attitude. Now you could be a slim person with a perfect BMI and a balanced diet, yet you still have pain. You'll will already know if it's because of a medical condition like scarring from an accident, operation or hereditary disorder. If it's none of the above, then your pain is or has been created by your past. I taught you in the opening chapters of this book, that your childhood and relationship with your parents, siblings and peers mattered in the first two decades. That decided how you will cope in your later years and connect with yourself. If you have not spent time in your past years working on healing your inner self, your body will store those negative emotions in your unconscious mind and in your muscle memory. Loss of relationships and never feeling good enough, will materialise as pain. That's why drugs won't make a difference. They only mask your need to self-heal.

Medication for pain relief will only take the edge off the discomfort; it cannot heal a broken heart, but you already know that.

As Mae West so profoundly said, "You only live once, but if you do it right, once is enough".

What she is saying is that you have a choice to live a full life. If you do it right, then you won't feel the need to come back and try again to get it right, because you did it right the first time round. You have a duty to you to become the best of who you are, not to live someone else's life or to save and rescue others. You need to save yourself first, then you can help others, by teaching them what you have learned about leading a successful and full life. Lead by good example. Choosing to focus on getting it right for you starts from now. Below is a short list of questions you can ask yourself. Use it to give yourself something positive to work towards.

1. **I have kept an open mind to new ideas and experiences** – As they say, a ship is safe in harbour, but that's not what ships are for. Accepting some level of risk in life is important. You cannot be both close-minded and wise. You have to open up to the unknown. Close-minded people who pretend to be wise to the ways of the world are mostly just cynics. Cynicism masquerades as wisdom, but it's the farthest thing from it because cynics don't learn anything. Cynicism is a self-imposed blindness, a rejection of the world that occurs when we're afraid it will hurt us or let us down. Cynics always say: "No". Do the opposite and say: "Yes". Saying "yes" is how things grow. Saying "yes" leads to first-hand experience and knowledge. "Yes" is for strong, open-minded people. So for as long as you have the strength to say "yes", please do.

2. **I am following my heart and intuition** – Don't be pushed by your problems; be led by your dreams. Live the life you want to live. Be the person you want to remember years from now. Make decisions and act on them. Make mistakes, then fail and try again. Even if you fail a thousand times, at least you won't have to wonder what could have been. At least you will know in your heart that you gave your dreams your best shot.

Each of us has a fire in our hearts burning for something. It's our responsibility in life to find it and keep it lit because it's far better to fail in originality, our own way, than to succeed in imitation every day of our lives.

3. **I am being honest with myself** – Be honest about what's right, as well as what needs to be changed. Be honest about what you want to achieve and who you want to become. Be honest with every aspect of your life, always. Because you are the one person you can forever count on. Own your choices, and be willing to take the necessary steps to improve upon them. Either you take accountability for your life or someone else will and when they do, you will become an instrument of their ideas and dreams instead of a pioneer of your own.

4. **I am making a difference** – Act as if what you do makes a difference. It does. Is it true that we all live to serve? That by helping others we fulfil our own destiny? The answer is a simple "yes". First, we live to serve ourselves and when we know ourselves, we can make a positive impact on someone else's life. Then that positive effect will impact on your own life, like a cycle. When you do something that's great, it helps someone else to be happy or to suffer less. You are only one, but you are the one that matters. You cannot do everything, but you can do something.

5. **I don't need anyone else to complete me** – There's far more to life than finding someone who will want you, or getting upset over someone who won't. There's a lot of important time to be spent discovering yourself without begging someone to fall in love with you along the way and this journey doesn't need to be empty or painful. You need to fill yourself with love, self-love you have learned by being good to yourself. Go on adventures, explore your passions, wander around the city and see new sights, sit in coffee shops and read, write a daily journal, leave notes in library books, dress up for yourself, give to others who can't pay you back, smile and have fun. Do all things with love, but don't worry about life. Once you give yourself love, you will feel healed and you will ultimately open yourself up to the possibility of healthy relationships with others.

6. **I have been brave enough to be vulnerable** – So many of us feel alone, even when we're surrounded by others we call friends and family. Inside, regardless of present company, we feel misunderstood and scared. We worry that telling people about our fears will make them think less of us. We wonder if anyone else feels the same way we do. We convince ourselves that we're weird, that no one else hears the voices in our head, that we're the only one who needs a hug. Well, wake up! You are not alone. Be brave enough to open up to those you love and you'll see that I'm right. Tear down any emotional brick walls you have built around yourself. Owning your story can be hard, but not nearly as difficult as spending your life running from it. Embracing your vulnerability is risky, but not nearly as dangerous as giving up on love and friendship and personal growth, all life experiences that require you to be the most vulnerable.

7. **I have forgiven those who once hurt me** – We've all been hurt by another person at some point in life. We were treated badly, trust was broken, and hearts were hurt. While this pain is normal, sometimes that pain lingers for too long. We relive the pain over and over, letting them live rent-free in our head and we have a hard time letting go. Grudges are a waste of perfect happiness; they cause us to miss out on the beauty of life. To forgive is to set a prisoner free and you discover the prisoner was you.

8. **I persevered through tough times** – Sometimes you have to die a little on the inside, in order to rise from your own ashes and believe in yourself in order to love yourself again. Call it growth. Call it finding yourself. Call it whatever you want. The key is to live moment to moment when times are tough and push forward, until moments become minutes, minutes become hours, hours become days, days become weeks, weeks turn to months, and time again has meaning. Life becomes worth living and the reason to smile. The process is almost like learning to walk or speak for the very first time. It isn't easy, but in the process we grow and we find ourselves, stronger, wiser and possessing talents we didn't know we

had. When we refuse to give up on ourselves, the hardest times can lead us to the best.

9. **I have no regrets** – This one is simply an amalgamation of the previous eight. Follow your heart. Be true to yourself. Do what makes you happy. Be with who makes you smile. Laugh as much as you breathe. Love as long as you live. Say what you need to say. Find the courage to feel different, yet beautiful. Find it in your heart to make others feel good too. Know that you don't need many people in your life, just a few great ones, so don't lower yourself and your standards for the wrong reasons. Be strong when things get tough. Remember that the universe is always doing what's right. Recognise when you're wrong and learn from it. Always look back and see how much you've grown, and be proud of yourself. Appreciate all the things you have. Celebrate your small victories. Forgive. And let go of the things you can't control.

Living the Good Life Pain Free

Many moons from now, when you're on your deathbed, what's the one thing you absolutely want to be able to say about yourself and your life? I know for me it will be:

"Thank you to me, for having lived a full live to the best of my ability. I have valued and appreciated everyone that has supported and loved me along the way. I have made the best out of every day I lived, every challenge that led to my growth, and embraced the things that have blessed and enriched my life".

Something along those lines should do it. Most of what I've just said is true, but the work never stops, when you are crafting an image of you. This image will be what remains of you, when it's your time to leave this earth. Therefore, I have still to face many more challenges that will lead me to an even better me. So when I'm gone, I will have left some small legacy that people will not only remember me by, for the good I hope, but something that they can use to become a better person. When you have achieved that, you have completed the circle of life.

If that feels like a mountain to climb, remember that life is full of jobs we never complete like the garden. Every season there is always something to do, even in the winter months it's all about preparation. The housework is unending, much like the ironing basket that continually grows. Your professional job (just like paperwork) never gets finished in the office so you take it home. You are a never-ending story, working on yourself is like a daily work of art, constantly in action. So don't complain if the garden, house or cleaning chores never get completed; they are just like you. In order to be the best you can be, you are a labour of love, eternally working on yourself until the day you leave this planet.

Here are a few things I learned along the way from my challenges, as well as from some great teachers. Add them to your journey to becoming the best of you:

1. **Beauty cannot be defined.** Beauty is a reflection of what you deem valuable. For me, it's an inner radiance and bliss that transcends judgement and fear, or at least makes an effort to.
2. **Perfection cannot be obtained** (and it's boring anyway). Trying to be perfect makes you feel inferior and desperate to change; owning your uniqueness makes you feel worthy and excited to evolve.
3. **Love will be messy at times.** Sometimes love looks nothing like it should or what you believed it would be. Unless you're in an unhealthy relationship, lean into the messiness. That's where the intimacy is.
4. **Other people will judge.** Doing your best and accepting that people will form opinions is far more empowering than stressing about what everyone else thinks.
5. **Sometimes there is no right or wrong.** There isn't always a right decision or answer. It's just about what feels right to you right now, and whether you have the courage to honour it.
6. **No one else knows what's right for you.** Someone else may seem certain they know what you should do. Should can

be deceiving; it seduces you with the promise of an ideal destination when what you really need is to choose for yourself and then pave your path as you go.

7. **Tomorrow is uncertain.** Despite all your planning, plotting, worrying or dreading, what will be will be and no matter how scared you feel right now, you can and will make the most of it.

8. **There are things you don't know.** And there are things you don't know that you don't know. It might be humbling to revise your understandings of things, but this is how you grow.

9. **No other person can make you feel whole.** Sometimes you feel a void and turn to other people to fill it. Mutually fulfilling relationships involve two whole people who complement, not complete each other.

10. **We can't change other people.** You have to want to change in order to do it. No matter how much you wish someone would act differently, it has to be his or her choice.

11. **There are some things you can't change about yourself.** Change sells (cosmetically) and it's seductive, but certain things cannot be changed, like parts of your body or nature. Love how you look - it's what makes you special.

12. **Sometimes there are gifts in the things we want to change.** For years I didn't like my low self-esteem and vulnerable emotions; now I channel them into something positive. Don't run from yourself; grow into yourself.

13. **You are worthy, just as you are.** Growth is a lifelong proposition, with no static endpoint. You do it not because you lack value, just as you are, but because you value yourself.

14. **You are going to age.** With every year that passes, we have 365 days to enjoy that age and no one age is better than another. Each is different, with its own challenges and gifts. So embrace it.

15. **You are more than any one role.** You are not one-dimensional and you don't have to be. Recognising this has been huge for me. I am a therapist and self-help writer who also likes

romantic comedy films, dancing and afternoon teas. I'm multifaceted and owning it!

16. **You are going to redefine yourself.** It's tempting to hold on to roles and ideas of who you are, but who you are is always evolving. Life's far more fulfilling if you see changes as adventures.

17. **You will occasionally have to do things you don't want to do.** You won't always love the things we need to do, for work or the people we care about, but we can find something enjoyable in it, if that's our intention.

18. **You will hurt at times.** Pain is inevitable. It's a sign that something's wrong with you, so you need to address the issue. It reminds you that you are human and your emotions will affect your mental and physical state. Have the courage to acknowledge your pain and work through it.

19. **You will mess up at times.** You will make mistakes and sometimes the same ones over and over again. This is a big part of how you learn. The important thing is that you do.

20. **People won't always forgive you.** You can't make someone stay in your life. You can only make amends and then be strong enough to accept the consequences of your actions.

21. **Peace is forgiving yourself.** You don't deserve to cower in shame and it won't do you any good. If you want to be happy, you need to cut yourself some slack and believe you are doing the best you can.

22. **You won't always like the consequences of your actions.** Sometimes you'll feel regret, wishing you could go back and do things differently. You can't, but you can make different choices going forward.

23. **You always have a choice in how you respond to what happens.** No matter what your circumstances, you can choose what you do with them. You can decide it's the end of the world, or start fresh from right where you stand.

24. **You are never alone.** It might feel like it, but there is always someone to offer love, kindness and support. You just need to be willing to reach out and ask for what you need.

25. **You will lose things and people you love but you can gain something from every loss.** Everything in life is temporary and no amount of time will feel like enough with the people you love. Loss hurts; you can heal if you believe it's possible.
26. **Everything is cyclical.** For every pain, there will be pleasure. Nothing stays the same, so relax through the tough times and fully enjoy the fun times. Everything transforms eventually.
27. **There are some things you may never understand.** Much of life is a mystery and its human nature to try to solve it. Peace is learning to embrace the open-ended questions.

Share Your Good Feelings with Others

What's the first thing you do when you get good news? You go and tell someone that's important to you, like a spouse or a friend. So you should treat positive events just like positive news. Tell another person when you are feeling particularly appreciative of a certain moment, whether it be a laugh with friends or a scene in nature.

Studies about the ways people react to positive events have shown that those who share positive feelings with others are happier overall than those who do not. In fact, research shows that one only has to think about telling others good news in order to feel happier. The saying goes, "You fake it till you make it". If people are unhappy and put a smile on their face, within an hour or so they'll be happier because they're getting smiled at by other people. That interaction works. Appreciation is the glue that bonds people together and it is essential for prolonging relationships. People who appreciate together stay together.

Take a Mental Photograph

Pause for a moment and consciously be aware of things you want to remember later, such as the sound of a loved one's chuckle, or a touching moment between two family members. In one study, participants, who took a 20-minute walk every day for one week and consciously looked for good things, reported feeling happier than those who were told to look for bad things. It's about saying to yourself, this is great, I'm loving it.

Congratulate Yourself. Pat Yourself on the Back

Don't hesitate to pat yourself on the back and take credit for your hard work. Research shows that people who revel in their successes are more likely to enjoy the outcome. This is not always the case throughout the world. Self-congratulation is not encouraged in all cultures, especially Eastern ones, where many individuals downplay their achievements or believe a good experience is likely to be followed by a bad one.

Sharpen Your Sensory Perceptions

Getting in touch with your senses or taking the time to use them more consciously will help heal the mind and body. With all the distractions we face today, finding a quiet moment can be difficult. In one study, college students, who focused on the chocolate they were eating, reported feeling more pleasure than students who were distracted while eating. Slow down when eating your meals. Take the time to shut out your other senses and hone in on one. Take the time to sniff the food, smell the food. Or close your eyes while you're taking a sip of a really nice wine. Tuning into your body is healing. Somatics is a therapy that uses this technique to allow the mind to heal the physical body from injury or recovery from surgery. It retrains the sensory nerves and muscles and heals from within.

Shout it From the Rooftops

Laugh out loud, jump up and down and shout for joy when something good happens to you. People who outwardly express their good feelings tend to feel extra good, because it provides the mind with evidence that something positive has occurred. Several experiments have found that people who expressed their feelings while watching a funny video enjoyed themselves more than those who suppressed their feelings.

Compare the Outcome to Something Worse

Boost positive feelings by reminding yourself of how bad things could be. For example, if you are late to work, remind yourself of those who may not have a job at all. Comparing good experiences with unpleasant ones gives you a reference point and makes your current situation seem better.

Get Absorbed in the Moment

Try to turn off your conscious thoughts and absorb positive feelings during a special moment, such as taking in a work of art. Studies of positive experiences indicate that people most enjoy themselves when they are totally absorbed in a task or moment, losing their sense of time and place, a state that psychologists call "flow". Children are particularly good at this, but it's tougher for adults, who are easily distracted by technology and the temptation to multi-task.

Recently, I discovered one task that really allowed me to be absorbed in the moment and that was gardening. Believe you me, I am NOT a gardener, due to the fact that I never have time (make time) to do any. I believe (falsely) that I'm rubbish with plants. In fact, I believe (again from past belief) that I kill plants so I don't garden. A few weeks ago, I was having a senior moment of meltdown and my husband asked me to go into the garden (it was an absolutely gorgeous sunny day which is rare in Britain) and help him deadhead a few flowers. He handed me a very small specialised (quite cute really) tool, that did the job. At first, I was like Richard Gere in the film, Pretty Woman. I was resistant to the new environment. I didn't want to be there; I had too much to do.

But as I slowly focused, on looking for the flowers that had died, my task was to clip the dead ones off so new growth would flourish. After five minutes, I felt so relaxed, as if the side of my busy brain had just shut down for a lunch break. The more I focused on doing the task in hand, the calmer I became (this is what happens during meditation, it's the same principle, but instead of focusing on the breath, I was focusing on the flower head).

That's why the gardener Monty Don wrote in his column and books, about how the soil in his garden was the best medicine for healing his Seasonal Affective Disorder and his recovery from his mini stoke. I knew what he meant. It was my epiphany, my moment of discovery. The garden is truly a healing gift the gods have bestowed on this planet. Those fortunate to know this gift are truly blessed. I now feel one of them. Gardening has always been associated with older people as they apparently have more time. It was what people did when they retired, but gardening is for all ages, the young and the old. It is a therapy in itself and is now used to help those suffering from all mental health issues, including dementia, as well as people on rehabilitation programmes.

Try to see what tasks help you do this in your day – pause and reflect on positive experiences on the spot.

Count Your Blessings and Give Thanks

Tell your loved ones how lucky you feel to have them, or take extra time to appreciate your food before a meal. Many people do this by thanking the lord for providing them with such a handsome plate of food. When many people around the world are starving, this is such a small act of thanks, but allows you to value what you have even more.

Research suggests that saying "thank you" out loud can make you happier by affirming your positive feelings. Why not think of a new blessing, for which you've never given thanks each night in bed? Recalling the experience through thanks will help you to appreciate it.

Avoid Killjoy Thinking

Avoiding negative thinking is just as important as thinking positively. After a rough day, try not to focus on the negative things that occurred. Studies show that the more negative thoughts people have after a personal achievement, the less likely they are to enjoy it. People who savour the positive sides to every situation are happier at the end of the day.

Remind Yourself of How Quickly Time Flies

Remember that good moments pass quickly, and tell yourself to consciously relish the moment. Realising how short-lived certain moments are and wishing they could last longer encourages you to enjoy them while they're happening.

In fact, when you value the positive moment, you can use it to connect you to the past or future. This can be done by remembering a good time and recreating it, or imagining a time in the future when you will look back with good memories. If you're working hard on a project, take the time to look at your accomplishment. Look at your experience and tell yourself how you're going to look into the future with this. Tell yourself, this is such a good day, and I know I'll look back with good memories. I did this with my own successes as well as with both my children's births, graduation days, 18th and 21st birthdays, even every holiday we loved together. I made moments in my memory so when I wanted to find a feel good memory, I could easily access them and feel happy again.

Motivational Quotes to Keep you Focused

"I will go anywhere as long as it's forward"
David Livingston

This is a quote that you can use each day to remind yourself that the best way to go is forward. There's no going back and there's no standing still, onward you go. So many times you can get lulled into a sense of comfort or complacency, but you have to keep the fires stoked and the engine moving.

This is a great way to sum up that you always want to be making progress and having fun things happen in your life. When you choose the direction you want to go, many times you get there.

"Positive anything is better than negative nothing"
Elbert Hubbard

It doesn't matter what it is as long as it's positive and it's something you can focus your attention on. You don't need to have dozens or hundreds of positive things taking place in your life at one time. You just need one positive thing that you can think about again and again to maintain your happy state. In fact, even if you have a bunch of negative things occurring in your life, you can safely ignore them all and just keep your mind on that one positive thing and all the negative things will work themselves out.

"Believe that life is worth living and your belief will help create the fact" William James

Belief is a powerful force and when you combine that with thoughts of a life worth living, you put into motion all of the pieces for a worthwhile life. Those who believe life isn't worth living will find that it comes true after a while. That's why it's so important to hold positive thoughts in your mind long enough until they become a belief. Only then will you be able to overcome all of the negativity that exists in the world.

SUMMARY OF WHAT YOU HAVE LEARNED FROM THIS CHAPTER

- **Fact**: Muscle Memory is a key player in allowing the body not just the physical functions it operates, but also balance, movement and speech. It has been designed to absorb our inner talking patterns through its sensory network system. From the moment you are born, every second your mind and body is learning, it uses procedural memory (the first step in how our body learns using the conscious mind) to learn motor skills. At the same time, it retains these skills through muscle memory, (used by our unconscious mind). It is here that our pain patterns begin to attach.
- **Fact**: Muscle memory is our automatic motor learning structure that allows our body to learn and remember how to walk, talk and run in order to function daily. It enables a baby to say its first words, a toddler to take its first steps, a child to ride a bike and a pianist to play Mozart. Thousands of sensory nerves that lay under every muscle group from the brain to your big toe communicate with the cerebellum at the back of the brain allowing this process to happen. It is like

---

a motorway network that allows our body to balance, move and speak. So if this network that controls our automatic skills and behaviour patterns through muscle memory exists, why is it so unbelievable that it listens to our internal conversations?

- **Fact**: Millions of sensory nerves that wire our mind and body together are like tiny transmitters that pulse repeated messages to form patterns, which our mind and body remember. It is through this internal unconscious instruction, that we are able to move automatically and function at such a high state, every waking second of the day. How you think, feel and speak to yourself daily has a profound effect on your wellbeing. When you repeatedly say the same thing over and over again internally and these messages are negative ones, then you are sabotaging your body, preparing for pain before you even know it.

- **Fact**: Negative messages delay recovering from any injury. Emotional and physical pain is therefore learned from birth, from the moment you enter the atmosphere, your mind becomes connected to the outside world and the people around you. Each decade you grow, your pain grows with you. Some people suffer great emotional pain during their childhood, which leads to physical illness in their early years. Whilst others suppress their emotions in childhood, leading to their ongoing battle with pain in middle age.

- **Fact**: When you rest your body it corrects itself. When you rest your mind it corrects itself. By being good to your mind and body, they will be good to you.

- **Fact**: Life is challenging and will continue to surprise you. Being prepared by having an optimistic outlook has been proven to support your wellbeing.

- **Fact**: According to the European Journal of Psychology it takes the mind 66 days to form a new habit.

WHAT YOU CAN DO RIGHT NOW TO CHANGE THINGS FOR THE BETTER

- Practise positive healthy thoughts daily from the moment you wake to the moment you go to sleep.
- The only person judging you is you. Stop the paranoia of not being good enough and start to showcase how brilliant you really are.
- For others to believe in you, you need to believe in yourself, then love follows.
- In order to form a new habit, you need to train the brain to focus on the new change. Daily repetition will allow your mind to focus on the new direction you want to take it. Soon you begin to think more in the positive mode, letting go of the negative.
- Get the right support team around you to help motivate your new direction. If it's a diet, join a group, if it's creative, select a course. If it's exercise, engage a personal trainer or friend to work out or walk with you. Get a journal to put your daily thoughts down, good or bad, happy or sad. Writing things down helps clear the mind, even if it's just a paragraph or a sentence, you are releasing stored pain.
- To become a champion and world class athlete it takes dedication, commitment and hard work. If you cannot give this to yourself, you cannot expect to get if from anyone else. When you commit to improving and healing yourself, you will cross the finishing line of life a winner and with that comes peace, happiness and a pain-free you.

FINAL WORD

"Learn from yesterday, live for today, hope for tomorrow.
The important thing is not to stop questioning"

~ Albert Einstein ~

I absolutely adore this quote. It simply hits the spot every time. In life, we don't always get it right, but that's the name of the game. As long as you do your best and keep trying, then that's all you can do. Isn't that what we tell our children today or grandchildren? Too many times people are quick to judge, to challenge, to question, to doubt and to persecute the innocent, the underdog, the one that always tried. It's not always about winning; it's what you learned along the way that counts.

You should never stop learning about who you are, what you want out of life and trying new things - that's what you are here to do. The world is a big, at times, challenging and dangerous playground, but don't let fear stop you exploring it. When you were young, you learnt through play, through falling a million times. Did you ever stop trying? No you didn't. If you did stop trying, then you wouldn't be able to walk, to run, to talk, to eat or drink. These are the skills you mastered as a baby so you could move forward, so what's the difference now? Age is only a number; it doesn't define a person. When you learnt as a child, you may have grazed your knee from time to time, but it made you more determined.

I remember learning to ride a bike. I loved my tricycle. I felt so secure with all those wheels on, but then my dad removed the stabilisers and my world caved in. I was so scared of coming off it, I froze. Although my dad was not a patient man, he did his best to encourage me to try and I did. I must have come off in every direction possible a hundred times, but I did it. How did I feel when I conquered it? Victorious! I was eight and I had nailed it. I became so good at it, that I, like my brother, entered the cycling proficiency test in our local town. I passed with flying colours. Even though my brother became West Yorkshire champion, I was extremely proud of him, but I was even more proud of me for trying.

We've all got such triumphant memories, hidden in our unconscious minds. You've just forgotten them and buried them deep in your box of achievements. It's good to take your 'trophies' out from time to time and give them a quick polish. They are there to remind you, not of how great you once were, but that you are still that same great person and with you, anything is possible. So get your map out, plan your route, raise the anchor and set sail to places that you have yet to discover. You are the captain of your ship, you are the master of your fate. You are that same remarkable person, still living your life to the full, enjoy the journey now voyager.

The Untold Want by Walt Whitman

The untold want by life and land ne'er granted, Now voyager sail thou forth to seek and find.

Invictus by William Ernest Henley

Out of the night that covers me,
Black as the pit from pole to pole,
I thank whatever gods may be
For my unconquerable soul.

In the fell clutch of circumstance
I have not winced nor cried aloud.
Under the bludgeonings of chance
My head is bloody, but unbowed.

Beyond this place of wrath and tears

Looms but the Horror of the shade,
And yet the menace of the years
Finds and shall find me unafraid.

It matters not how strait the gate,
How charged with punishments the scroll,
I am the master of my fate,
I am the captain of my soul.

REFERENCES

Introduction

- *Scientific Evidence-Based Effects of Hydrotherapy on Various Systems of the Body* research paper by A. Mooventhan and L. Nivethitha National Centre of Biotechnology Information (NCBI) 6th May 2014

Chapter One

- *'The National Right To Life Educational Trust Fund'* Washington DC Factsheet.
- Dr Stuart W.G Derbyshire, University of Birmingham 15th April 2006 - Can fetuses feel pain?
- Colleen A Malloy M.D Assistant Professor in the Division of Neonatology Department of Paediatrics Northwestern University Feinberg School of medicine - Testimony before the Subcommittee on the Constitution on the District of Columbia Pain – Capable Unborn Child protection Act (H.R. 3803).
- Dr. Marisa López Teijón and Dr. Álex Garcia-Faura – paper on 'Fetal response to Music in the Womb' published in NCBI Ultrasound Journal of British Medical Ultrasound Society.
- PNAS (Proceedings of the National Academy of Sciences) - 10th September 2010 paper on 'Learning - Induced neural plasticity of Speech processing before birth authors Partanen. E, Kujala. T, Litola. A, Sambeth. A and Huotilainen. M

- Dr. Thomas Verny Association for Prenatal and Perinatal Psychology and Health (APPPAH - The Secret Life of the Unborn Child).
- Dr. Deepak Chopra *Magical Beginnings, Enchanted Lives*
- Bruce Lipton, Ph.D Cell Biologist and Neuroscientist – The Biology of Belief

Chapter

- Bolwby J. (1980). *Loss: Sadness & Depression. Attachment and loss (vol. 3)*; (International psycho-analytical library no.109). London: Hogarth Press.
- Raikes, H.A. & Thompson, R.A. (2006). Family emotional climate, attachment security and young children's emotion knowledge in a high risk sample. British Journal of Developmental Psychology, 24(1), 89–104.

Chapter Three

- The Teen brain still Under Construction - NIH Publication No. 11-4929 2011
- Kotulak, Ronald. *Teens Driven to Distraction. Chicago Tribune*. March 24, 2006.
- Powell, Kendall. *How does the teenage brain work?* Nature. August 2006.
- Wallis, Claudia. *What Makes Teens Tick?* Time. May 10, 2004. (Aug. 12, 2008) *www.time.com/time/magazine/article/0,9171,1101040510-631970,00.html*
- Monastersky, Richard. *Who's Minding the Teenage Brain?* Chronicle of Higher Education. Jan. 12, 2007.
- For more information on conditions that affect mental health, resources, and research, go to *www.mentalhealth.gov* at *www.mentalhealth.gov* , or the NIMH website at *www.nimh. nih.gov*.

Chapter Four

- Paper on *Twentieth Century Mortality Trends in England and Wales* by Claire Griffiths and Anita Brock Office for National Statistics.

- Sheldon B.Kopp author of *An End to Innocence.*
- Erik Erikson *Insight & Responsibility* (1964)
- Source: U.S Bureau of the Census 2007 – Marital status
- Cochrane Report - Meditation for anxiety disorders - Krisanaprakornkit T, Sriraj W, Piyavhatkul N, Laopaiboon M. 25th January 2006
- Stanford School of Medicine Research paper on OCD – Department of Psychiatry
- Paul Angone Author of *101 Secrets For Your Twenties'* and *All Groan Up: Searching For Self, Faith, and a Freaking Job!* Anxiety UK – General Anxiety Disorder (GAD)

Chapter Five

- Ralph Marston *The Daily Motivator – www.greatday.com*
- Dr Marilyin Glenville book *Fat Around the Middle.* Amazon
- James Horne Loughborough University Sleep Research Centre *Mobile phone 'talk-mode' signal delays EEG-determined sleep onset Study* - 24th May 2007.

Chapter Six

- Research paper entitled *Is Well-being U-Shaped over the Life Cycle?* By Professor Andrew Oswald, Department of Economics, University of Warwick 28th January 2008
- Office for National Statistics (ONS) on late mother's in their 40's having a baby.
- *Up, Not Down: The Age Curve in Happiness from Early Adulthood to Midlife In Longitudinal Studies* - a paper by University of Alberta researchers Nancy Galambos, Harvey Krahn, Matt Johnson and their team.
- Sane Mental Health Charity – *www.sane.ork.uk*
- Sainsbury centre for mental health publications
- Dinges, Sleep, Sleepiness and Performance, 1991
- Van Dongen & Dinges, Principles & Practice of Sleep Medicine, 2000
- Division of Sleep Medicine at Harvard Medical School and WGBH Educational Foundation. (n.d.). Consequences

of insufficient sleep. Healthy Sleep. Retrieved from *www.healthysleep.med.harvard.edu/healthy/matters/consequences*
- National Sleep Foundation. (n.d.). How much sleep do we really need? Retrieved from *www.sleepfoundation.org/article/how-sleep-works/how-much-sleep-do-we-really-need.*
- 2014/2015 HSE (Health & Safety Executive) Statistics
- *Call the Midlife* by Chris Evans Amazon
- Information on Prostate cancer - *www.prostatecanceruk.org*

Chapter Seven

- *The Secret* book by Rhonda Byrne
- United Nations International Children's Emergency Fund, UNICEF - *www.unicef.org.uk*
- The American Society for Aesthetic Plastic Surgery – 20th March 2014 statistics
- *Woman over 50 warned not to avoid smear tests* -NHS Choice publication 15th January 2014
- Pulse paper for GP's in the UK published 18th April 2004 an analysis of the Women's Health Initiative, showed a possible risk reduction in women taking oestrogen - only HRT who were aged 50-79 and had a hysterectomy.
- *www.ageuk.org.uk*
- Study by researchers from University of Birmingham on water and weigh loss - published 28th August 2015
- University of California Study on Alzheimer's delayed with HRT 2013 - funded by the US National Institute on Aging and the National Institutes of Health.
- Amy Hackett-Jones - Life & Leadership Coach & Speaker | High-Performance & Happiness | Being Brilliant | TEDx Speaker
- Bereavement Charity Cruse - *www.cruse.org.uk*

Chapter Eight

- *Optimism, coping, and health: Assessment and implications of generalised outcome expectancies.* By Scheier, Michael F.; Carver, Charles S. Health Psychology, Vol 4(3), 1985, 219-247.
- The Office of National Statistics (ONS) Report 2002 to 2014 on Estimates of the Very Old (including Centenarians): England and Wales, and United Kingdom, 2002 to 2014
- *www.independentage.org*

Chapter Nine

- Dr Mary Newport Coconut Oil & Alzheimer's Report
- *www.dememtiauk.org*
- Science Direct paper on *Exercise, experience and the aging brain* James D Churchill, Roberto Galvez, Stanley Colcombe, Rodney A Swain, Arthur F Kramer, William T Greenough. October 2002
- Alzheimer's Association
- Harvard Medical School
- Mayo Clinic
- National Institutes of Health
- National Research Council and Institute of Medicine
- Lissa Rankin, MD, New York Times bestselling author of *Mind over Medicine, The Fear Cure* and *The Anatomy of a Calling.* The Whole Health Medicine Institute - *www.wholehealthmedicineinstitute.com*
- Dr Bernie Segal author of *Love, Medicine & Mircales*
- *The Good Gut: Taking Control of Your Weight, Your Mood and Your Long Term Health* By Justin Sonneburg and Erica Sonnenburg PhDs.
- Optibac probiotics - *www.optibacprobiotics.co.uk*
- *It's All in Your Head* book by Dr Suzanne O'Sullivan

Chapter Ten

- *www.weightwatchers.co.uk*
- *www.slimmersworld.co.uk*
- Somatics Therapy - *www.somatics.com*
- Book – *The Jewel Garden- A Story of Despair & Redemption* by Monty Don & Sarah Don available Amazon
- Camilla Sacre-Dallerup Life Coach, Hypnotherapist & meditation Teacher *www.zenme.tv*
- Amy Hackett-Jones Peace, Power & Purpose Coach *www.amyhackettjones.com*

Printed in Great Britain
by Amazon